SPIRITUAL TEACHINGS OF THE AVATAR

SPIRITUAL TEACHINGS OF THE AVATAR

Ancient Wisdom for a New World

Jeffrey Armstrong
illustrated by Farel Dalrymple

ATRIA BOOKS
New York London Toronto Sydney

 BEYOND WORDS
Hillsboro, Oregon

ATRIA BOOKS
A Division of Simon & Schuster, Inc.
1230 Avenue of the Americas
New York, NY 10020

BEYOND WORDS
20827 N.W. Cornell Road, Suite 500
Hillsboro, Oregon 97124-9808
503-531-8700 / 503-531-8773 fax
www.beyondword.com

Copyright © 2010 by Jeffrey Armstrong

Managing editor: Lindsay S. Brown
Editor: Julie Steigerwaldt
Copyeditor: Mary Ann Jeffreys
Illustrations: Farel Dalrymple
Design: Devon Smith
Composition: William H. Brunson Typography Services

First Atria Books/Beyond Words hardcover edition June 2010

ATRIA BOOKS and colophon are trademarks of Simon & Schuster, Inc.
Beyond Words Publishing is a division of Simon & Schuster, Inc.

For more information about special discounts for bulk purchases,
please contact Simon & Schuster Special Sales at 1-866-506-1949 or
business@simonandschuster.com.

The Simon & Schuster Speakers Bureau can bring authors to your live event.
For more information or to book an event, contact the Simon & Schuster Speakers
Bureau at 1-866-248-3049 or visit our website at www.simonspeakers.com.

Manufactured in the United States of America

10 9 8 7 6 5 4 3 2 1

Library of Congress Cataloging-in-Publication Data

Armstrong, Jeffrey.
    Spiritual teachings of the avatar : ancient wisdom for a new world / Jeffrey Armstrong ;
    illustrated by Farel Dalrymple. — 1st Atria Books/Beyond Words hardcover ed.
        p. cm.
    Includes bibliographical references.
    1. Spiritual life—Hinduism.   2. Avatars (Religion).   I. Title.
    BL1237.34.A76   2010
    294.5'44—dc22
                                                                        2010013430

ISBN: 978-1-58270-281-0
ISBN: 978-1-4391-9702-8 (ebook)

The corporate mission of Beyond Words Publishing, Inc.: *Inspire to Integrity*

TO THE ALL MOTHER,
ALL MOTHERS,
AND MOTHER EARTH,
MAY ALL THEIR CHILDREN BE
FED, SAFE, AND HAPPY.

THE TREE OF ETERNITY

With twigs that stretch out toward infinity
And branches reaching to touch eternal light,
This universe is the boughs of a mighty tree,
Holding all life in the shade of endless night.

While ages of time color the countless leaves,
Galaxies burst forth as its golden seeds,
Watered by tears, it grows when someone grieves,
Blooming with flowers; perfumed by our needs.

Blossoms that turn to fruits of pleasure and pain,
Salty, sour, bitter, pungent, and sweet,
Fire, air, earth, and water as rain,
Roots dug deep in space, like ancient feet.

This is the mighty Oak, the Banyan, the Pine,
A seed from a cosmic wind, blown from far away,
The trunk on which each soul is a clinging vine,
In the garden of love that answers when we pray.

And peace is the gentle breeze that waves each bough,
Beneath Father Sun and Mother Moon, this tree
Is the symbol of Truth to which we all should bow,
In the forest of life, stands the Tree of Eternity.

Jeffrey Armstrong
(Kavindra Rishi)

CONTENTS

Acknowledgments

Writing a book is a collaboration of many kinds of genius. In a great film like James Cameron's *Avatar*, five minutes of credits allow us to see the names of the many people whose skills and services gave life to the final result. I wish we could do the same with this book, but here we must be more concise—I thank all the Devas and Devis I've undoubtedly missed. You'll know who you are.

First, to my guru, His Divine Grace A. C. Bhaktivedanta Swami Pradhupada, and to my many gurus and teachers from India: I bow to you for your generosity in passing the Vedic knowledge to me with the wish that it reaches those who hunger for divine wisdom. Then, to all the elders of Indigenous cultures who have taught me—may your wise voices be heard throughout the world. Next, to my love and life partner, Sandi Graham, who like the Great Goddess Herself has twenty arms reaching in all directions doing everything at once. She is my muse, whose wisdom and love are everywhere in this book.

Then there is my friend, editor, and other right arm, Pete McCormack, who stood by this text like Lakshman with Ram, attracting the Devas of brilliance and chasing away the asuras of error. Our editor and proofreader, Richelle Jarrell (Richelle Devi), polished the text like a gem for Sita's hair. Our typists and content readers, Matthew Granlund, Ellen Huse, and Pia Shandell, gave of their time and abilities most generously. And thanks to Anthony Kuschak (Garuda Das), who with great skill and dedication managed and held together the platform of our lives while we wrote this book. Thank you to our students and friends for their blessings and constant devotion to this great knowledge.

Amy Armstrong and Sherry Butler of Armstrong Troyky Public Relations both had their magic hands in the making of this book. Our reader from India, Abhijit Phadnis, acted as the voice of Bharata, a connection to the root of the tree. Special thanks to Chief Jake Swamp for sharing his story of the Liberty Tree. Thanks to Shaun Bradley and Don Sedgwick, our literary consultants at Word by Word Publishing Services.

This brings us to the other amazing team who shaped and cocreated the beauty of this book—the many hands and eyes at Beyond Words Publishing, headed by Cynthia Black and Richard Cohn. Their combined keen insight, universal vision, and dedication to excellence decorate every page of this book. To Dan Frost, their acquisitions assistant, whose keen eye and steady hand held all the many parts of the project in place. Their managing editor, Lindsay Brown, and editor, Julie Steigerwaldt, brought both the artistic and textual work to a world-class level. The graphic artist, Farel Dalrymple, worked miracles in re-creating the visions from the great epics, while our graphic designer Devon Smith, created a gorgeous cover, inviting our readers to look within. Finally, to the many brilliant hands and minds at Simon & Schuster, who in myriad ways made this book possible. Last of all, we thank the trees who gave their bodies to carry the messages of the Avatars—we will personally plant five more trees in their names.

And, of course, thank you to the All Mother, Gaia, Mata Bhumi, Mother Earth, who inspired and manifested this book—we're looking out for you.

NOTES ON LANGUAGE CONVENTIONS

In this book, we have followed certain conventions of capitalization and usage that reflect the philosophical viewpoint of Vedic and Indigenous cultures. The following words are capitalized: Avatar, when used as a synonym for the Supreme Being; Sanskrit names for the Supreme Being or Reality; the Transcendental as a place considered to be a Divine realm; Nature and the Divine beings who assist Her; the planets, including Earth, which are treated as Divine beings with proper names; the Laws of Entropy, or Science, and the Laws of Nature; and our Universe, when referred to in the metaphor of the Cosmic University.

Words such as Source, Universal Intelligence, and Feminine Divine are capitalized just as God would be. Yoga, when referring to any Vedic process for reaching the Divine, is capitalized just as the name of a specific religion would be. When referring to yoga postures, yoga is not capitalized. Aboriginal and Indigenous are capitalized as categories of people, just as citizens of a specific country would be.

The library of Vedic knowledge is referred to as the Vedas or "as the Vedas say," and the first time a Sanskrit word is used, it is italicized.

INTRODUCTION

Paradigm-shifting ideas can germinate for years, even decades, until the time is right for them to manifest. So when I heard that it took over twenty years for director James Cameron to develop the vision for his recent megablockbuster film *Avatar*, I was not surprised. Although I do not have a personal relationship with Mr. Cameron, we do have something in common: I have spent the last forty years studying the deepest meanings of the word *Avatar* and the multilayered teachings associated with it. I was, in fact, teaching a series of classes on the subject of Avatar when, to my surprise, a student recommended I see a film called *Avatar*.

I saw the film in IMAX 3D and was greatly inspired by Mr. Cameron's expansive cinematic vision. Within days, a cascade of events was set in motion. During my daily meditation practice, I had a vision of the book you are now reading. Less than a week later, my publisher and I agreed on a book contract.

James Cameron's choice of the word Avatar—a key word from the Divine stories of ancient India, and my special field of study—inspired the writing of this book at this precise moment. *Spiritual Teachings of the Avatar* is dedicated to revealing the deeper meanings contained in the concept of Avatar. Behind the film and this book—and many undeniable trends unfolding at this time in history—are the will and working of something greater. One can call that will the All Mother, Mother Earth, Gaia, Divine Spirit, or whatever you like, but its existence should be clear to anyone even remotely aware that the human species and the planet we inhabit are at a watershed moment.

Both the film and the book converge on this historical moment, when what we do next could affect positively—or tragically—all life on our planet. Through science and technology, we have grown too powerful to continue the unconscious and at times irresponsible use of our resources and abilities. We are at a crossroads where we must somehow learn to more deeply cooperate with one another and chart a course for the future that includes the safety, dignity, and well-being of all living entities. Unless we do so, we risk catastrophic consequences, militarily or environmentally.

As I walked out of my first viewing of *Avatar*, I turned to my wife, Sandi, and said, "It appears that Mr. Cameron has opened Pandora's Box Office." I'm prone to such puns. In Greek mythology, a young girl named Pandora is given a box by her father, who cautions her not to open it under any circumstances. Her curiosity, of course, eventually gets the better of her, and she opens the mysterious chest. Out flies every manner of pestilence, problem, affliction, and misery. Just as it seems all is lost, one last being emerges from the box: luminous, quivering, and sensitive—that being is Hope.

Seeing *Avatar*, I felt that sort of hope for a sometimes cynical and endangered world. It was the same hope I experienced forty years earlier when I was initiated into the life-changing wisdom of the Avatars by my teachers from India. It was the same hope to which I have dedicated my life. That hope is actually a lifestyle based on a set of teachings that are the treasure of the best Indigenous cultures on our planet. As you will see from this book, India and the many noble Aboriginal cultures have been the historical keepers of the secrets of living in greater harmony on the Earth. The word *aboriginal* means "with the origin"—in other words, "awareness of the original intention" of life. Undeniably, aspects of that original intention have been skillfully woven into the fabric of the film *Avatar*. However, what I want to do here is reveal to you the original and expansive meaning of the word Avatar—and what the deepest meaning of that word offers. And so it is with deep appreciation for James Cameron that this book is being written. By titling his box-office smash *Avatar*, Mr. Cameron both borrowed one of the most important spiritual words in the history of India and simultaneously helped give rise to the opportunity to tell its real meaning.

The movie *Avatar* shines a glaring light on some of the oppression, unchecked greed, and injustices we see happening around us today. The movie's message is perhaps most relevant for those profit-only corporate heads who behave as if taking from the world, without concern for the consequences, is their right—and one justified by the earnings garnered for their shareholders. This attitude needs to give way to a caring corporate ethos with heart, balanced somewhere between sustainability and profit.

I also hope that *Avatar*'s message can be heard by the institutions that try to force their religions on other people and erase their cultural heritage in the process. It is time to usher in the day when all people throughout the world practice religious and cultural tolerance as an essential part of their religions.

The movie could also be seen as a call against despotism and dictators of all types whom we see leading undemocratic nation-states all over the world. How can we be serious about being free if we *all* are not allowed to speak freely?

Another important issue raised by *Avatar* is the meeting of technological science with Indigenous science. In other words, how can we advance technologically without going against Mother Nature's vast intelligence? How can we even come to believe in an intelligence that to so many is self-evident? Answers to these big questions are what the Hope in Pandora's Box is asking us to ponder.

As a teacher of the Transcendental for forty years, I'd like you to know that it is with great humility—and yet a palpable excitement and joy—that I invite you along on this paradigm-shifting ride. In the coming chapters, we will explore in great detail the further meanings of the *Avatar*'s more subtle and important teachings, and the connection between Avatars and India's two great epics, the *Ramayana* and the *Mahabharata*, in much more intimate detail.

A color insert beautifully depicting scenes from each of the two epics has been included, and at the back of the book you will find guided meditations, practices, and chapter summaries that will help you more fully absorb the profound teachings of the Avatars.

It is my sincere wish that *Spiritual Teachings of the Avatar* will provide tools of knowledge that help you live and be your most authentic self—whatever your worldview—and that this book will inspire and encourage you to help solve personal, local, and global dilemmas through greater consciousness, cooperation, and integrity. The Avatars are unequivocal about one thing: with the correct vision, we can, starting today, begin to fulfill the promise of Hope that remains in Pandora's Box and, most important, in the deepest, kindest, most courageous parts of our own hearts.

In guiding you, I offer my eternal gratitude and deepest respect to the extraordinary elders of so many Indigenous cultures from whom I have learned and, of course, to my gurus and teachers in India who shared with me the real treasures of the Avatar tradition in the hope that we yet can learn to live in greater joy and compassion on Mother Earth.

ONE

NAMASTE—I SEE YOU

*Namaste, I see you as a beautiful Divine being whose
eternal consciousness pervades your body and mind,
and is the light of your true self, shining across to mine.
I bow to that transcendent being that is the real you.*

Albert Einstein, the great intuitive scientist of the twentieth century, said, "Imagination is better than knowledge." Knowing this instinctively, our Indigenous ancestors taught through multi-layered stories in which information was carefully embedded and imagination was a prerequisite. These ancient stories often had a dream-like quality, which films such as *Star Wars*, the *Lord of the Rings* trilogy, the Harry Potter series, and *Avatar* use to take us into their imaginary worlds. To get the full effect, the listener has to temporarily turn off the critical mind and open the heart. Similarly, to be closer to the traditional way Indigenous knowledge was transmitted through storytelling, the teachings in this book need to be absorbed like an internal movie. To do this, I ask your help. As challenging as it is in this hyperknowledge modern world, I need you to set your critical mind aside until the end of the book. Sit back, set your analytical thoughts aside, and get as comfortable as a student beneath a banyan tree thousands of years ago, so you can take in this learning through an open heart. To do so is not to accept it—it's simply necessary to truly hear it. Just as with your own life, with this knowledge you are the cinematographer, special-effects person, and set designer, but not, yet, the film critic.

And in this moment, I, too, will transform myself from a regular person, a product of the culture in which I was born, into an elder from an ancient and wise culture that remembers the oldest stories from the beginning of time. I do this with humility and confidence, because this stance is my truest nature. Like Jake Sully "died" at the end of *Avatar*, so Jeffrey Armstrong also "died" forty years ago, was filled with a new vision and purpose, and in the process was reborn and renamed. Since that day, I have lived and worked in the hopes of restoring the vision of a healed, healthy, and sacred world. Now, I humbly ask the Avatars to speak their wisdom through me, that I may be their emissary and ambassador to you, and share their vision with you.

Definitions

Before we begin, I would like to give you definitions of three key terms that will really help you hold the *Spiritual Teachings of the Avatar* in the right context. The terms are *Vedic Library*, *Transcendental*, and *Avatar*.

Vedic Library

The Vedic Library is synonymous and will be used interchangeably with the Vedas. Over many thousands of years, a large body of learning called the Vedas accumulated in what was once called Bharata and is now called India. Written in the precise Sanskrit language, some of the Vedas are said to have been directly downloaded from higher realms to yogis (on Earth) in deep states of meditation. Other books are said to have been spoken by the great Avatars who came to Earth. Others are histories that stretch back millions of years. Many volumes describe the Laws of Nature, science, arts and architecture, astronomy, astrology, medicine, language, etymology, philosophy, and—more than anywhere else in the world—stunning descriptions of Transcendental realms beyond our sight where, it turns out, only our deepest desires can take us.

None of the books in the Vedic Library is attributed to a specific author, although many are identified by their compilers. In *Spiritual Teachings of the Avatar*, when I write, "The Vedas say," I am repeating ideas directly from the great Vedic Library. In a more academic situation, the speaker would likely quote precise chapter and verse. Here, instead, we are delving into the sweet spirit of the teachings.

Transcendental

Connecting with the Transcendental requires both a softness of heart and a sharpness of mind. The Vedas tell us that we are currently living in one of several energies that could be the basis of existence. We are in the material world, or realm—and our Universe is only a small part of the total material realm. The energy of matter is inert, unconscious, made of parts, temporary, dark, and always expanding and contracting.

Everything within matter manifests, lasts for a while, and then is broken down and recycled. It is this material reality that we are used to experiencing. However, the Vedas also say that matter is only one quarter of the greater reality. The other three quarters exist—beyond our sight—as the Transcendental. In contrast to material reality, the Transcendental is fully conscious, dynamic, eternal, self-luminous, and without parts, and experiences no duality or opposition. It is the essence of our truest nature. The Transcendental is also a place. It precedes our Universes of Matter, is always expanding, and knows no death, disease, limitation, or time.

By this definition, the Transcendental may seem inconceivable to us, as we are so used to being in matter. The Vedas tell us that we are eternal beings who chose to come here from there and can also choose to return to our original Transcendental home.

Avatar

Avatar, a Sanskrit word, combines *ava*, meaning "to descend," and *tara*, "to heal and restore." The idea is that a divine being, or Supreme Being, purposely descends to Earth, takes on a body (which appears to us as a person being born), and then fulfills some kind of mission according to the needs of the moment. This is different from reincarnating, which is not a conscious, intentional birth but a result of karma. The Avatars come according to their own will.

When the Avatars come, their primary purpose is to rescue and heal the Earth at a time when the balance in Nature or Mother Earth is being destroyed. The secondary purpose is to remind us that we also are beings from the Transcendental and that transcendental is our true nature. The Avatars usually leave us a set of teachings that are essential tools for living a life of integrity for the good of all. The Avatars exemplify this message and teach us to do the same. Thirdly, the Avatars come to develop personal and loving relationships with humans in a number of different flavors: as servant, child, friend, spouse, or lover. In the process, humans get to interact with the Avatar—in simple terms, God or the Supreme Being—who has lovingly come to us disguised in what appears to be a human form.

Although the knowledge I am about to project onto the screen of your imagination first appeared in the place we now call India, no person there claims ownership or authorship. It has been received over millions of years by thousands of people—and woven into the stories of great Avatars. It is everyone's and no one's. You may take freely from it as you need or reject it as you wish. With my feet in the roots of antiquity and my head in the branches of today, our story begins.

In the Service of the Avatars

My reborn name, bestowed upon me by a great teacher of the ancient wisdom, is Kavindra Rishi, which translates as "one who hears and speaks the ancient wisdom." I will be your guide on this journey. I am an elder in the ancient lineage of wisdom, received in Bharata, the region we now call India. We are the keepers and carriers of a library of knowledge, which is called the Veda, or Vedas. The English word *video* comes from the word *Veda*, which means, "to see and realize the truth." The Vedas have traveled through time in the Sanskrit language, which means, "the perfected language," and has kept the meaning of our knowledge from being distorted or lost over time. I will be introducing new Sanskrit words and revealing new meanings for English words. This is necessary because, according to the ancient Vedas, certain Sanskrit words were actually designed by the great seers and sages of the past to convey pictures and deep experiences in very precise ways. Sanskrit words are considered a kind of spiritual programming language that by its sound alone expands our imaging capabilities. In a sense, these words create special effects within us.

How is that open heart feeling?

We Are Eternal Beings Called *Atmas*

The truth of all the ancient cultures is that they understood that we are eternal beings who are visiting this Universe. That is why when they greet one another, they say some variation of "I see you."

In Sanskrit the word is *Namaste*, which means "I see you as an eternal divine being." This is the universal spiritual greeting that says, "I am looking past your clothing, body, skin, culture, ideas, personality, even your thoughts, and I see the real you inside, visiting here on the Earth Campus of a Great University."

According to the timeless and ancient Vedas, this Universe that we live in is but one of countless billions of similar Universes—and science has shown this ancient teaching to be true. The word *Universe* means "one reality turning" or "one unified revolving reality"—a single field of entirely interconnected energy that manifests, continues for a period of time, is recycled, and then manifests again. It is the Vedas that describe each of these Universes as a sort of university—a campus to which unlimited numbers of eternal beings come to learn from the school of matter. These Universes are actually described as the material aspect of the Supreme Being, which is the reason we're attracted to coming here in the first place. Living here in the material Universe, the Vedas say, are 8,400,000 material bodies, or grade levels, that the Supreme Being manifests—from microbes all the way up to human beings—all of which we as eternal beings will inhabit at some point during our evolution through matter. And each one provides a specific experience required on our path toward eventual graduation.

This eternal being that came to Earth is called an *atma*. This atma is our true nature. To be clear, "being eternal" means we were never created and we can never die. I can only tell you that humans who finally get this become a lot more relaxed about their current state of material affairs—which is remarkably hard to do, it turns out, even with this knowledge.

Atma Vacation

At some point in this eternal journey, an atma decides to migrate into the material world and begin its studies at the University of

Matter. When that atma comes into contact with matter, two things happen. The atma immediately believes it is matter—not the atma that it truly is—and this new material-spiritual alchemy of a being begins to breathe air. The Sanskrit word for an air-breathing eternal being is *jiva-atma*.

Again—and the great sages have told us this for thousands of years—we can be neither created nor destroyed, and when we arrive here, we simply begin to evolve by experience through one type of physical body after another. This, of course, is the essence of reincarnation. We are climbing an evolutionary ladder through matter, through the millions of species, from the most simple to the most complex. Each experience is a grade level that peaks at the human experience, where for the first time we can be truly self-reflecting, asking who we really are.

And who we really are is the atma.

The atma is eternal, conscious, joyful, and individual by its true nature. To repeat, we are not human beings; we are not these bodies; we are not even our thoughts. We are eternal beings temporarily covered in material bodies that we incorrectly believe to be us. Put another way, we are individual atmas having a human experience, not humans having a spiritual experience.

And according to the great teachers, we don't come from here either. Where we come from is called the Transcendental realm—which is also, after we have fully experienced this material world, the place to which we will one day return.

Again, the atma itself is not material but is the same in nature and quality as this Transcendental realm. The world—and all of us as materialized beings—is made of an unconscious energy called matter. The antimaterial, or transcendental material, is made up of a conscious, eternal energy. By comparison, this material world is dark and inert. The Vedas tell us:

The Transcendental world is self-luminous.

This material world is temporary; the Transcendental world
    is eternal.

This world is static; the Transcendental world is ecstatic.

This world is full of anxiety; that world is free of anxiety.

Further, the Transcendental world is also, inconceivably and simultaneously, here and there. Veda reveals the Transcendental world to be our original home. And for the record, we are not talking about heaven. From the yogic point of view, heaven is a very enjoyable and more subtle material dimension that is still temporary. The Transcendental world is utterly beyond the material world.

Universal Education

The implications of this grand vision—that all living entities are at their core eternal, conscious, joyful Divine beings or atmas—lead to a universal code of conduct and a context in which to see the evolutionary process of all that lives. It is not true that we are evolving consciousness as a result of chemical reactions within matter. We are not bubbles from random and inert matter. Neither are we temporary creations of a whimsical or anthropomorphic deity. We are all beings who live forever. There was no time in the past when we did not exist, and there will be no time in the future when we cease to exist. By analogy, our atma is just like the sun, which is situated in one (moving) place yet radiates its light throughout our solar system. Our atma—who we really are—is also shining the rays of its eternal consciousness into our minds and bodies.

This is true for all beings—all species—without exception. One who understands this greets every being with the same "Namaste—I see the real you." This greeting should be the standard greeting for all students who are aware of the purpose of this Universal Campus.

Seeing all fellow beings, all students, correctly, is a vital first step toward more cooperative, caring-for-the-good-of-all behavior on the campus of planet Earth. Although in different grades, often because of the differing times of our arrivals, we are still all the same in essence and are here for the same reason. All students are equally valuable and worthy and should be seen and treated with the same respect. The question after the greeting of "Namaste," even if asked silently, should be: "What grade are you in?"

This grading, of course, through our modern scientific classifications, has largely been done for almost all of the visible and even microscopic beings on our planet. All have been categorized into grade levels according to their habits and abilities. Compared to the human potential, all the species below us are currently confined to the lower grades of evolutionary learning. Their habits and habitats are restricted, and their self-awareness is not as expanded as ours is. On the campus, we might say that they are in grades K–12. The ability to fully self-reflect, and accordingly the development of free will, is not yet available to them. This is not an insult. This is a factor of time. They are still young souls.

Free Will Is Not Necessarily Free

The Vedas tell us that the difference between human students and the younger souls who almost exclusively use only instinctive consciousness is the use of free will. This use of free will—which is possible because we are atmas—is the link between the atmas, the laws of matter, and the evolutionary process we are going through. Up through the highest mammals, but before our human experience, the atma's ascent takes place without the use of moral free will. Although animals have autonomy within the boundaries of their species, they cannot step very far outside the limits of their bodily natures. For this reason, we do not think of nonhuman creatures as bad or good in the same way we judge humans. There is actually no such thing as, say, a bad bear; bears are just atmas in bear bodies—having bear experiences. The same is true for all creatures up to the level of humans. All unconscious or habitual creatures are controlled by the Laws of Nature in the same way all matter is—through cause and effect. Even we humans suspend our use of moral law until children reach a certain age. Only then do we think people are morally accountable for their actions.

The greatness and privilege of reaching the human experience is that for the first time we can actually ask who we really are. Discovering who we are—the atma, and not these physical experiences we have been having—is one of the keys to what is called liberation or in Sanskrit *moksha*. Realizing we are not these bodies provides the opportunity to return to our true home—the Transcendental—as well as to our true nature—as the atma.

The difficulty, upon reaching the human level of experience, is that for the first time after millions of lifetimes, we have, as the saying goes, minds of our own. As a result of having minds that can consciously or even accidentally act contrary to the Laws of Nature, we become not only accountable to the physical laws of action and reaction in matter, but also responsible for our moral behavior that results from our use of free will. This process of cause and effect—where the results reflect back to humans for what we do with individual free will—is called *karma* in Sanskrit. Whether one sees these reactions as good or bad is irrelevant to the Laws of Nature—certain actions have a price, whereby a cause, perhaps immediately or at some future date, will result in an effect. It is never punishment, merely cause and effect.

In contrast, according to the Vedas, all plants and animals reincarnate in an inexorable, upward movement toward human birth. Once we reach the human experience, however, this instinctive, built-in control mechanism is relaxed, and free will becomes the determining principle for our advancement. In fact, if we behave badly enough—for instance, by not using our human faculties—we can even return to a limiting animal birth whose nature we, for whatever reason, desired to imitate while we were in human form. To put it in terms we've all heard, what goes around comes around. But more deeply, what we desire, we ultimately get. In ways our minds can barely grasp, we humans think and speak everything into being with our thoughts and words. The world is reshaped by our thoughts and words, which we should always strive to refine. This process is immediately elevated by seeing a more expansive vision of who we are.

Samsara: The Cycle of Repeated Births and Deaths

It is important to understand that karma is neither punishment nor reward; it is simply the rules within the curricula of this Cosmic University. In this process, it is good to remember that there is no such thing as eternal punishment. Such an idea is completely contrary to the desires of both the atma—no matter how down on ourselves we get—and the Avatar, whose deepest wishes are in the coming chapters. The purpose of the school is a full experience that moves the transmigrating atma students toward graduation—toward a reunion with their original home. All karmas are temporary—meaning the results of our actions produce temporary effects—although, to us, with our smaller vision, it can feel like the effects are going on forever.

The point is, since all the atmas are eternal and here to learn, it is free will that gives the school and its classes meaning. What stays with us is the wisdom we acquire, which builds gradually until we are eligible to graduate.

During the entire journey through the lower species, the atmas are in a sense "dunked under" by contact with matter; they forget their eternal Transcendental nature and believe that they are only bodies. They are unaware that the body is a temporary condition. Among humans, it takes lifetimes of human learning to finally grasp that we are not bodies or minds, but rather we are eternal beings whose consciousness is operating our minds and bodies.

In all beings, their unconsciousness that they are eternal beings makes them automatically resist death and dying. After all, the atma does not really die, but when its body starts to die, there is a natural struggle against the process. In humans, this "fear of death" or aversion to it continues until we are "old souls," meaning we do not forget from moment to moment that we are not bodies. In the film *Avatar*, reincarnation is demonstrated by Jake Sully's going back and forth between his Na'vi body and his human body. In this case, his eventual jump from a paraplegic human body to an empowered Indigenous leader demonstrates reincarnation in action. In Jake's case, he consciously chooses to change his mind and then change bodies before our eyes. The key point to remember here is that the countless atmas are controlling their own physical bodies with the light of their consciousness that is emanating from their atmas. If the idea of seeing everyone as an atma sounds simple, I can only tell you it is not. This truth is a profound step to seeing past our external differences and leads us to truly appreciate what we all have in common. That we are all atmas is not only what connects us to all human beings, it is also the secret of our connection with all forms of life. We are all atmas: eternal students on the same campus, here for the same purpose. In this way, we are all valuable, divine in essence, brilliant in nature.

TWO

THE MOTHER OF ALL

Namaste, I see you as part of everything, deeply connected to all that exists.
I feel your love and good wishes for all beings.
Your compassion washes over me like the waves of a loving ocean.

Take your mind back to just over five thousand years ago. Mother Earth is deeply worried. Many evil beings have taken birth in India and are living disguised as kings in royal attire. They pretend to be noble but secretly are fostering evil and causing great harm. Their large and vicious armies harass everyone. Women are not safe, taxes become intolerable. Just as we sometimes feel today, for our ancestors in India, all appears to be lost.

With tears of compassion for Her children, Mother Earth takes the form of a cow and travels to the Creator of All, Brahma. She tells Him of Her sadness, and He suggests an emergency visit to the Supreme Being, Vishnu, the protector of all, to ask for His help. When they reach Vishnu's realm, Vishnu explains what is going on:

"My beloveds, I have sent those evil kings to Earth to set the final stage for My own descent to Earth as an Avatar. Very soon, I will

13

personally appear, to restore and teach the balance of life. Please instruct all the divine helpers to take birth in royal families. My revelation is imminent."

And so came the wisdom, compassion, and courage required to restore balance to Earth and to dry Mother Nature's tears.

The essential operating principles of Mother Nature—the All Mother, Mata Bhumi—are renewal and balance. All great Indigenous cultures understood this relatively mathematical secret: if the good of all is to be a possibility, leaders must attune themselves to a sacred balance with one another and the immutable force and intelligence of Nature. To anyone willing to listen, Mother Nature's endless output and desire for the sustenance of all beings on the planet is a true marvel to behold.

Famed scientist and environmentalist Dr. David Suzuki has estimated that Mother Nature annually provides over thirty trillion dollars of economic output, free of charge, and we don't even believe She exists, let alone protect Her. She is constantly breathing to restore the campus to balance so that it can benefit and serve the journey of the endless waves of incoming students. She is a thermostat and a soft bed; she is the most thirst-quenching drink and the fragrance of love. She mends, weaves, rearranges, recycles, and rebirths all through the mysterious layers of life's genius fabric. And given that humans have the most free will of all beings, it is we among all biological life who can most easily be the cause of environmental imbalances or, even worse, have complete ignorance of Her as a living, breathing, utterly selfless Divine. And within that spectrum of free will also lies the possibility of collective understanding of our utter dependence upon Her—and how Her secrets are revealed by listening, not by forced extraction. This dependence, we need to understand, is not mutual. Mother Nature can continue in our absence.

Honoring the Devas, the Divine Helpers

The Vedas describe themselves as a manifestation of the Divine Mother, helping us understand both the male and female forms of truth as well as their profound and inseparable union. And the Avatar in human form describes the three groups of beings in the Universe: the nonhuman creatures; humans of course; and, finally, the seemingly invisible and largely forgotten divine helpers—forgotten despite their endless efforts on our behalf. In Sanskrit they are called *Devas*, and they work on behalf of the Supreme Being in the ongoing maintenance of the Universe and as the manifestation of the Laws of Nature. Deva, which is the root of our English word *divine*, means "playing in the light." From other Indigenous cultures, they have come to us with countless names, such as angels, spirits, faeries, gnomes, and the wee people.

It is commonly understood that Indigenous cultures have always viewed the Earth as a great being that is alive in every sense of the definition—and far greater than ourselves. How did they discover this? Put another way, how did we forget this? They also understood that Mother Nature did not do Her work alone but employed billions of divine helpers to assist in the biosphere's ongoing renewal. From the viewpoint of the Supreme Being or the Indigenous shaman, the divine helpers are seen as Divine beings. From the point of view of science, the Devas remain unseen but are evident as the Laws of Nature. Either way, the process is infinitely beyond genuis or personhood, as we comprehend it.

From the Vedic point of view, the divine helpers are both beings and the personified Laws of Nature. Just as the police, for example, personify the laws of the city and assist in its running.

At any given moment in the atmas' education within matter, some are having the creature experience, some are having the human experience, and some are having this Deva experience. Devas, like us, are atmas, but in lighter bodies and unable to exercise free will as we can. Their function is selfless service. Just try to imagine a personification of the outpouring bounty we receive. Through this idea we can begin to rebuild the idea of a relationship between us and the environment, between eternal atmas having a human experience and a great atma—who is having the experience of being Mata Bhumi. Imagine for a moment what we receive every day to sustain us—through no work of our own and no awareness. To envision this generosity from the All Mother is to begin the birthing of gratitude in our hearts.

Of the many ancient teachings that the movie *Avatar* reintroduces, the clear expression of the All Mother's beauty, tenderness, and generosity is one of the most needed, and most welcome. That Her film debut was created in a studio on green screens, using advanced technology is all the more remarkable, and a little ironic. However it was done, Her promotion in our hearts and minds—and into our imaginations—is being applauded by many Indigenous cultures. In the absence of this vision, this sensibility, we have seen a couple of centuries of violent and rapacious thugs trampling the planet and destroying its treasures, including the irreplaceable knowledge of a natural pharmacy—plants, seeds, and herbs—and the death of countless species forever, as if there were and is no All Mother witnessing our every action. Her return into our collective psyche, and our hearts, is long overdue.

The point is twofold. First, those who have celebrated their awareness of and belief in the Mother of All have historically been unnecessarily suppressed and marginalized—even killed. This is totally against the Indigenous worldview that says every individual should be free to choose a relationship with the Source of his or her existence without any threat of force or coercion. Second, could modern science's inability to personify Mother Earth be the reason behind its insatiable desire to manipulate Nature's output in ways that discard the inherent balance and wisdom of Her processes? The powers unleashed by this impersonal view of life are a grave danger to our most personal requirements: water, air, and food. Those who see Her resources only as matter feel they have a right to take what they will. To those who see Her as an organism deserving reverence and relationship, this is straight-out vivisection. Which is correct?

Avatars of the Devas

As we drive certain plants, animals, and resources to extinction, a scene in *Avatar* symbolizes the hopeful epiphany for modern technology when scientist Dr. Grace Augustine finally sees the All Mother Eywa and says, "I can see her, Jake, and she is real." What would it look like if science and business—and our own habits—supported a more sustainable planet? Would the economy really collapse from a reduction in fossil-fuel use? What if the same urgency we applied to war or bank bailouts or races to Mars were applied to the manufacturing of renewable-resource technology?

On our journey here, how can we children of Nature be complete without a loving relationship with the All Mother in Her many forms—along with the All Father? Although in the Abrahamic religions the Divine Mother does not exist as part of the story, in the Vedas the Divine Mother is the true sustainer. She is the inseparable Shakti, or energy of the male. And just as a human mother would care for all her children, so the Mother of All Nature and Mother Earth does not favor one group of Her children over another. If our conscience cannot be awakened by wisdom or common sense, then devolution resulting from our insensitivity to environmental change—a lack of resources to sustain ourselves—remains the Great Mother's prerogative. And if She's not a being, with whom are we negotiating? With whom are we gambling? And if She is a being, what pain She must feel when children needlessly go hungry? Part of the Hopes in Pandora's Box is that modern science decides to join with the deepest traditions of our ancestors to reimagine our world as a peaceful and sustainable place for the safety and growth of future generations.

In the face of apparently unstoppable destruction, how brave can we be? The Vedas also describe the Avatar of Devas who take birth as humans. For example, a Deva might be born into a human family to lead humans in a time of crisis. Almost all Indigenous cultures have stories about extraordinary beings being born into their tribes—beings who inspired them to new levels of peace and cooperation with Mother Earth. Those great people probably were Avatars of a Deva, divinely sent by the All Mother.

Whatever the truth is about this wondrous yet inconceivable reality in which we find ourselves, we know our home planet, Mother Bhumi, is in some ways fragile and finite, but is also constantly expressing to those who will listen the kind of stewardship that could lead to a better life for more beings.

We are here to learn these long-term, wide-cast lessons of cooperation. Your mother had a mother, who had a mother, who had a mother, and so on, back to the Mother. Your father had a father, who had a father, all the way back to the Father. Having Divine parents should not seem any more difficult to fathom than is the reality of having human parents.

Reverence. Gratitude. Relationship. Attunement. All these atmas—dressed as variously shaped beings, as we are—are simply passing through on the process of rediscovering our highest natures and finally remembering who we are, all while studying the Divine beauty and intelligence. For this reason, humans are implored by the Avatar's teachings to leave the planet in perfect condition for the next generation. We need to listen, for nothing could be more ignorant than destroying everything by urgently strip-mining for what is ultimately unobtainable.

The process of sustainability can be deeply enriched through really trying to feel what a relationship with Mata Bhumi—Mother Nature—might look like. On this spiritual journey, trying to live more sustainably can be a means of increasing one's consciousness while surrounded by matter. Listen inward. Listen to all that surrounds you. The tears you cry for the environment, both joy and sadness, are the tears of your Original Mother. You are feeling Her, and She is feeling you—and you both know it. How beautiful is that?

home tree and ecology

*Namaste, I see you standing straight and tall, reaching your
truthful branches to the skies of possibility. You are ripe with the
fruits and flowers of abundance for which we are so grateful.
Together we breathe the balance of life into each other's lips.*

Lf life on our planet were today as it had been for tens of thousands
of years, this story of the Avatar, of sustainable coexistence,
would be told *under* a tree instead of being written *on* a tree. In addition, the tree being sat beneath would simultaneously be a metaphor
for the teacher to convey multiple layers of Universal truth.

Indigenous cultures understood the value of trees in ways the
modern world, for all its advancements, is just beginning to
reawaken to. Indeed, looking at etymology, words like *truth*, *true*,
and *trust* all arise directly from the word *tree*. The progression is *tree
→ troth → truth*. The relationship becomes obvious upon hearing the
root meaning of tree: "standing straight and tall." If you *believe* your
truth, then your truth is covered in your *beliefs*, or in your "be-leaves."
By literally digging into the "roots" of language, how the ancients felt
about trees begins to be revealed on multiple levels: physically, spiritually, and psychologically.

Avatar wisely places the great Home Tree at the center of the cinematic discussion. Through the ages, many Indigenous cultures have told important tree stories. The sharing of these tree stories promoted a holistic process by which their truths could be integrated—a sort of photosynthesis in the ground of our earthy being. The goal was an awareness of how to live sustainably on the Earth.

Trees inhale our carbon dioxide and exhale oxygen, which we inhale. This intimate relationship is the essence of life and its importance was not lost on our ancestors. Poetically speaking, just as lovers breathe the air from each other's lips, the trees and humans are constantly giving each other mouth-to-mouth resuscitation. The trees' "blood" is green chlorophyll, while ours is red hemoglobin, ever-cyclical, pumping, in relationship to the very inhale and exhale of life breath. In a world of exponential technological expansion, the reality and symbolism of this ever-present, ongoing relationship between humans and trees is critical to our survival.

Money: The Root of All Trees

Until recently, our standard for truth as well as our standard of living on planet Earth have been intertwined with trees. Our cyclic relationship to weather, day and night, and the changing seasons has been obscured by the widespread use of fossil fuels. Indigenous peoples cultivated the forests in which they lived, listening constantly to the whispers of Nature. With such an intimate relationship to Earth, Indigenous peoples knew that each year one could only extract a certain quantity of energy without causing damage to the forest ecosystem. The "living capital" of their lives was the forest, while their "income" was the amount of food and fuel energy that could be extracted each year. In spite of the remarkable advances resulting from our use of nonrenewable fuels, our relationship with trees and the cyclic rhythms of Nature has been badly damaged.

In his classic book *Small Is Beautiful*, E. F. Schumacher has a chapter called "Buddhist Economics," in which he describes how Buddha recommended each of his followers plant *one tree every five years to replenish the energy they had consumed*. This is the kind of thinking India has tried to maintain throughout Her history. Glimpses of this wisdom remain in many places.

In Kenya, Nobel Prize–winning Wangari Maathai literally revived large areas of devastated Kenyan land by replanting millions of native trees, in spite of much opposition. Unlike silviculture groups and pulp-and-paper industries that plant only one kind of species in a large area, a practice known as monoculture, Maathai was specific about the need for correct trees being planted in the correct places. In sync with her ancestors and Indigenous wisdom, Maathai knew that the trees, soil, and underground springs all had a collective memory—and so she planted accordingly, even though she often risked her life to do so. The Avatar comes to reawaken our connection to Nature in order to bring ecosystems back to balance.

Originally, wealth was food or small amounts of other valuables harvested, hunted, or gathered from Nature. In a pre-money world, the barter system of trading goods was the essence of economics. Even with the arrival of paper money, currency was often backed by silver or gold or some other precious commodity. Money's value was not dangerously arbitrary. This backed-currency system has slowly weakened over time. Paper money today has no relation to real wealth or assets but is merely fluctuating promises printed on paper.

Our confused relationship with paper money is in dangerous lockstep with our imbalanced relationship with Nature. Just as our money is a promissory note "guaranteeing" something that is constantly decreasing in value, our addiction to fossil-fuel extraction—or at least the products resulting from that extraction—is promising what can never be fulfilled: infinite resources. Wealth in the previous centuries of life on Earth was found mostly in the tangible fruits of photosynthesis from the plant kingdom, with a profound awareness of finite resources and the cyclic nature of all things. Following the metaphor in the film *Avatar*, our modern promissory notes may well be shares in a corporation selling *Unobtanium*.

IQ, WeQ, and Now 3rd IQ (Third Eye)

The greatest barrier to integrating the wisdom of Indigenous cultures into our modern life is the misunderstanding that these cultures were primitive and unscientific. Science has two basic methodologies: one is logical/mathematical, the other is intuitive/direct perception. The Indigenous renewable culture was less technological and more intuitively perceptive. The Indigenous worldview is based on listening to Nature and making certain that extraction and renewal are in balance. Technological science uses a controlled and detached process to reach its conclusions. Intuition is more a direct seeing that goes straight to the conclusion, skipping the intermediate steps. These two processes are sometimes loosely described as left-brained (logical) and right-brained (intuitive), or IQ (Intelligence Quotient) and EQ (Emotional Quotient). In our technological IQ-driven world, EQ and emotions have been given little respect. This is ironic since paradigm-shifting scientific conclusions like Newton's theory of gravity, Einstein's grasp of relativity, and so on were mostly intuited. Intuition has been marginalized as more soft and feminine for millennia. The development of modern science followed a mathematical path toward truth, in a sense making math, logic, and experimentations its prejudice. This pushed intuition into the background, leaving IQ as the standard definition of intelligence. Our schools still test the IQ of children mostly according to their abilities in math-based logical skills. Those less competent in IQ are often dismissed as less intelligent.

In *Avatar*, we see a collision of IQ and EQ worldviews. Indigenous cultures have focused on intuition as their preferred scientific methodology. Our modern scientific methods, for all their wonder, are seriously distorted and are leading us to a precipice of imbalance. Indigenous cultures were keenly observant intuitive scientists whose direct observations led to rich relationships with the environment. IQ science excels in dividing and extracting, while EQ science excels in listening and cooperating. Perhaps IQ and WeQ is a better pairing since the left-brain "I" dominates the world, whereas WeQ favors cooperative integrating methods. Both IQ and WeQ learning are necessary, but clearly we are out of balance due to too much IQ focus. The teachings of the great Avatars show how to harmonize IQ and WeQ with a third faculty called 3rd IQ (Third Eye). This knowing is connected directly to Universal Intelligence through special kinds of perception contained in the Avatar teachings.

For now, we are at a global tipping point where Indigenous/intuitive listening and mathematical/logical doing are in critical need of mediation and reconciliation. Included in this schism are the so-called liberal (meaning right-brained) and so-called conservative (left-brained) political parties. Seen from the 3rd IQ perspective, they have some common ground but are inclined to be extreme and unbalanced, and thus they are missing the necessary strengths in the other. Balance has been lost, and balance is one of the essential teachings associated with the Avatar. The goal of the Avatar is always to restore humans' balance with Nature so as many beings as possible are working for the good of all life.

Balancing Entropy—Capturing the Sun

To fully understand the human-tree relationship, it is necessary to understand one of the pivotal laws that informs all science. Aboriginal scientists understood these laws intuitively—just as they have now been proven mathematically by modern technological science. The central law of all matter is encoded in modern science as the Law of Entropy, which arises from the two Laws of Thermodynamics.

The First Law: Matter (energy) is never created or destroyed; it simply changes form.

The Second Law: All matter is going from a higher state of energy to a lower state of energy (entropy) and is in the process giving off both heat and waste.

In simple terms: there is no such thing as a perpetual-motion machine. This is the perception at the center of all sustainable Indigenous cultures. This same law of modern science was expressed in the Vedas of India for many thousands of years. Matter is a limited resource, it is cyclic, and using energy exhausts the resource in the production of a predictable amount of heat and waste. To simplify, envision all matter as having three transforming states: full of energy, releasing energy, or empty of energy.

The nature of matter is to capture a certain amount of solar energy each year. Using that energy creates useful power and waste that must be recycled. Modern science knows of this process but has ignored its implication by adopting a nonrenewable energy source. So far no one has ever produced unlimited energy with no waste. Our supply of nonrenewable energy is limited, and by burning too much of it too quickly, we have upset the balance of our planet. With no indication that the fundamental Laws of Nature will change or can be fully ignored, it is obvious we need to start listening to the Indigenous techniques for working with the cycles of nature.

As far as we know, we are the first humans on Earth who have so deeply distorted the cyclic and rhythmic process of gathering our annual, sustainable quota of energy from Nature and Her finite resources. We are on track to extract and burn all of the stored fossil-fuel-energy resources available on planet Earth. We have no solution for this problem and no commitment to try to solve it. At present, as with our economic debts, we are simply ensuring a legacy of indebtedness and unredeemed waste for our own children. By departing too far from the Indigenous, cyclic model of living, we are dangerously close to extracting all of the energy capital of our planet—capital that took millions, even billions, of years to produce. Many experts predict this epoch-ending moment of fossil-fuel depletion is fifty years or less away.

In *Avatar*, James Cameron gave this energy source, upon which the Home Tree existed, the perfect name: *Unobtanium*. The analogy with today is obvious: we have traded our intimate relationship with the trees and the cycle of seasons and the finite resources for a belief that some infinite Earth-found resource will be discovered at the last minute, saving us from a return to cyclic reality.

Branching Out

The vision of the Home Tree in Indigenous cultures was not only vital to everyday existence but was also a symbol for teaching the subtle truths of the world—anatomical, physiological, and metaphysical ones. Our circulatory system, in its progression from arteries to veins to capillaries, resembles the tree as it progresses from trunk to branches to stems to leaves. Our lungs also mimic this branching structure. Our nervous system, rooted in the brain, reaches out treelike in a chemically mediated network that, in remarkable detail, has long been known to the ancients. A second treelike system, running parallel and powered by direct-current electrical signals rooted in the brain stem, was also known and mapped by direct, intuitive science and was called the acupuncture meridians. Energy and signals that direct the healing processes of the body run down these meridians, or energy pathways. In modern times, there are point locators that find the acupuncture meridians by means of electronic resistance. The points are exactly where the ancient scientists intuited them to be.

Celtic cultures, and Druids in particular, revered the oak tree and the mistletoe growing upon it as the living symbol of all interconnected life. For the same reason, the Scandinavian cultures of northern Europe depicted the Universe as a great tree, which they called *Yggdrasil*, or "World Tree," another teaching tool for the web of life. The holy text for the Indigenous Scandinavian culture was called the *Veddha*, undeniably similar to the Vedas from India.

In the Indian Vedas, the tree is also depicted as a pivotal symbol for all life, including the forest, as sacred. Sages and forest-dwelling monks have for millennia sought the silence and purity of deep nature for all forms of worship and meditation. Monasteries, ashrams, and universities were strategically placed in sacred forest sanctuaries. Especially in a warmer climate, forests could produce all the food needed throughout the year, making a vegetarian existence possible for long periods of time.

Of all trees, one of the most remarkable is the tropical banyan tree. This tree, along with its already massive roots, has huge branches that eventually reach the ground, send down roots, and in time become new tree trunks. In a way, the tree grows beyond description: branches go down, the center is everywhere, the roots are endless. There are banyan trees on record in India that are over a hundred feet tall and cover more than ten acres. The banyan tree with "roots and branches reaching everywhere" is described in the Vedas like the cosmos and so has long been a symbol of the Universe in Indian thought. The great forests of the Amazon, which are in parts being deforested at a terrifying rate, are also famous for such trees.

In *Avatar*, James Cameron combined images, truths, and customs from many ancient cultures. Similarly, practitioners of the Vedic path honor the wise elders of other Indigenous nations. I learned a story from an elder and chief of the Wolf Clan of the Mohawk Nation, from the Iroquois Confederation of Indigenous Peoples, who lived in the eastern United States and Canada. His name is Chief Jake Swamp, founder of the Tree of Peace Society, which is guided by the principle of thinking seven generations into the future.

According to Chief Jake, around a thousand years ago, the Indigenous peoples in the eastern region of North America were constantly at war. The price was horrific: endless suffering and fear, with many wounded, crippled, or killed. Peace was nowhere to be found. Then a special being took birth in one of the tribes. As he grew to manhood, his personal qualities were so compelling that he eventually became a chief. His wisdom and strong desire for peace eventually inspired all the nations and tribes. Finally, he called them together and gave them a plan for living in peace.

He proposed the digging of a very deep hole into which they all would throw their weapons. He then arranged for a huge pine tree to be planted above the weapons. As soon as the tree was planted, and in the presence of all the tribes and their leaders, a large bald eagle landed on top of the tree. Since that time, the tree has been called the Tree of Liberty. This Avatar then taught the Iroquois people the concept of representative government, where every year all of the tribes would send representatives to a designated place and votes would be taken to decide uniform rules of living. The Avatar further instructed that women would select the Iroquois tribal leaders, and to prevent war, the wise woman of the tribe could choose and remove leaders if necessary.

This idea of representative democracy, of course, took place some seven hundred years before Europeans came to the Americas. According to Gregory Schaff, in his book *The U.S. Constitution and the Great Law of Peace: A Comparison of Two Founding Documents*, the secret not being taught in schools throughout the world is that democracy and representative government were deeply influenced by the Iroquois elders. Jake further told me that the Iroquois records show the Iroquois Constitution and the U.S. Constitution to be strikingly similar, and that a month prior to the writing of the U.S. Constitution, a delegation of Iroquois elders went to the capital to advise the Founding Fathers in their forming of a nation.

We can only hope that the replanting of trees and a more balanced relationship between IQ and WeQ ways of living are the next phase of our development. The Tree of Liberty is ultimately based in balance and cooperation. The Avatar shows us that on a global scale, the tree needs to be replanted and restored as a symbol of our truth and well-being.

FOUR

ENERGY IS EVERYTHING

Namaste, I see your life force flowing like a crystal stream down a mountain.
The vibrations of your electric body and healing energy fill me
with inspiration and joy. You were never created,
and you cannot be destroyed.

Indigenous cultures approached the Earth with an attitude that was based in recycling and transformation. An ancient yet well-known Taoist saying states, "In this world the only constant is change." Our logical, IQ-driven, ownership-oriented, technological world is largely run on the energy of money. The wealth of WeQ-oriented cultures—cooperating with Mother Nature, borrowing but never really owning—was the energy of the life force itself.

In Sanskrit, the life force is called *prana*, the Chinese call it *chi*, and the Japanese call it *ki*. And just as *Avatar* has popularized components of ancient wisdom, its epic predecessor, *Star Wars*, did the same by opening the modern world to the invisible but ever-present Force. In short, matter can be owned temporarily, but the Force always owns us. We do not breathe it; it breathes us. It belongs to no one and is imminently and freely available everywhere. As it was spoken in *Avatar*, "There is a network of energy that flows through all living things. It is borrowed and someday you must give it back." Unlike the more tangible realm of matter—which at least *appears* to belong to us but is in fact temporary—prana cannot be grasped or owned. This energy is a free resource of Nature, literally the vital force of Mother Earth's body. With very little effort, we can learn to cultivate more of this energy, and with it heal or prevent imbalance.

The Sanskrit word *prana* is also found in the English word *animal*—*pranimal*—which is an onomatopoetic version of our in-and-out breathing process. Both we and the plant realm, led by the forest, are constantly breathing life into each other. The gases and energy carried by the plant realm support our life force, which supports the physical components of our bodies. Unprocessed foods, pure air, pure water, and the proximity of plants are the main sources for our life force. Highly processed foods, bottled water, and polluted or air-conditioned environments without vegetation are largely void of this vital life force. Unreported by modern technological medicine, many people today suffer physically and mentally from being starved for *prana-vitality*. We are literally cut off from the purest, vital sources of life that were known to all Indigenous cultures.

About fifty years ago, what has been long known in India, China, Japan, and Korea about this vital life force finally began to reach Western minds. The path has not been easy. The most orthodox of the IQ crowd still deny its existence. Only in the last twenty years has technological science become subtle enough to actually measure and thus "validate" this invisible force, and the energy-based arts are today spreading rapidly throughout the world. What has become well-established is this: parallel to the chemical-based nervous system is a direct-current electric healing system of meridians, or *nadis*, as they are called in Sanskrit, that constantly flood the body with prana, much like an irrigation system waters a farmer's field. This movement of pranic energy can be altered or enhanced by herbs, foods, massages, acupressure and acupuncture, special exercises like chi gong that are designed to facilitate its flow, hands-on energy transfer from one body to another, special yogic breathing methods called *pranayama*, and by many other ancient techniques.

The current revolutions in vegetarianism, organic gardening, natural foods, yoga, tai chi, chi gong, and many martial arts and similar lifestyle practices are all based on pranic healing. These techniques are by definition contrary to many of the foods, medicines, and products developed by material science for large food and drug producers who are either unaware of or uninterested in the healing qualities of the life force–enhancing substances. This resistance is predictable. Our use of fossil-fuel energies for hundreds of years has created remarkable products by harnessing Earth's energy, but it has also suppressed our inherent connection to Earth's (and our own) cyclic energy rhythms. In the industrialized regions, night and day, the influence of the seasons, and local food sources have been largely unplugged and neglected. Where these shifts have damaged our life force, all too often money-making chemical medicines have taken the place of less expensive healing herbs. The renewed global popularity of Yoga and the revival of Ayurvedic preventive medical teachings from India, based on cultivating and protecting the life force, are signs of restlessness with the chemical quick fixes of emergency medicine. India, China, and many other cultures have ancient herbal pharmacopoeias with thousands of safe and well-documented preventive energy-full medicines.

Unfortunately, pharmaceutical corporations, emergency medical practitioners, and processed-food corporations have either exploited or overlooked Indigenous healing science. In contrast, the Ancient teachings are emphatic that health-promoting lifestyle science focused on prevention is the basis of all social well-being. Those sciences are rooted in the enhancement and cultivation of one's life force. It would be most accurate to label this preventative medicine through the healing use of better food, herbs, and lifestyle. Industrial food production is more and more complicit in the rise of chronic lifestyle-caused diseases, which in turn make universal healthcare a financial impossibility. No culture can afford the price of healthcare if its citizens are fed an assembly-line diet of devitalized food.

Patient, Heal Thyself

Food conglomerates have made a science of both artificial food and propaganda, creating the illusion that factory-created, time-saving, busy-lifestyle foods are better than their organic, biodiverse, and unprocessed counterparts. The truth is that the industry focuses on creating multisensory experiences, using massively processed foodstuffs and artificial flavors and unnecessary amounts of refined fat, sugar, and salt. These experiences create addiction by working on the part of the brain known as the *mesolimbic reward system*—just as illegal experiences such as heroin and cocaine work on the drug addict. Modern processed food in its vast proportions literally reshapes our brains.

The simple truth—or *tree-uth*—should be obvious: foods and supplements made from natural plant substances, sustainably cultivated or found in forests and meadows, are *the* preventative and healing medicines proven most effective for thousands of years.

The understanding of prana, or energetic state, as the definition of health demands that we live together as if we are connected parts of the same body. In the film *Avatar*, the entire tribe holds the same worldview, that the All Mother/Mother Nature/Bhumi/Earth is the conscious and ever-active Being Who integrates all life. It is Her energy flowing through all of life, and She cares for all of life.

We are meant to live in a prana-rich environment, to be touched, massaged, affirmed, embraced, and honored by and connected to the flow of life energies. But in our modern and fragmented world, in cities with millions of people, loneliness is a big problem. People often live sad lives—untouched, unseen, unheard, and uncared for. This harms their prana and hastens disease by lowering energetic levels and weakening the immune system. Caring female qualities arise from maintaining an active loving relationship with Mother Earth. All Indigenous peoples were in constant communication with the All Mother and Her helpers, and they touched each other a great deal. In losing this contact and connection, we have succumbed to a world of inert matter, breathing bad air and eating manufactured foods delivered from machines and made in factories without real nutrition, let alone light and love.

In the ancient stories of India and many other cultures, the appearance of the Avatar is always a "descent to heal and deliver" the world from beings who are endangering all life. In the same way our bodies have a protective immune system supported by prana, the immune system of Mother Earth is protected from time to time in history by the descent to Earth of great heroes who fight any evil that would harm the innocent or injure the life force. According to the ancient teachings of the Avatar, we are cells in the body of Mother Earth and each cell can choose to be the solution or the problem. The outcome will be decided one cell at a time. By listening, we can decide to be a helper cell in the All Mother's body. By listening, the Force, so to speak, will be with us at this crucial time in history.

Today, we are ideally positioned to combine the remarkable advances in emergency medicine and physiological understanding with the pranic healing sciences. The obstacle is always human greed, which should have no significant place in a healing and compassionate endeavor like medicine. Excessive profit from human sickness and suffering has become its own form of social disease. The Avatars taught that all humans should have enough nutritious food to eat and that medical care is not a business but a divine service.

Therefore, it is not competition between various styles of healing that should engage us but rather a relentless search for whatever works to prevent illness in the first place. In order for this to happen, the life force–increasing sciences need to be integrated with our modern emergency medicine and its sterile medical environments. Both our health and our healthcare system depend upon it. When this happens, the signs will be obvious: First, the hospitals will serve healthy, organic food; the rooms will be ventilated with fresh air; and the hallways will be populated with more healers than surgeons. Second, there likely will be less need for hospitals.

In the Vedic teachings of the Avatars, the interrelationship among the physical body, the energy body, and the mental body has been highly developed. In modern terms, it could be in part described as the physics of sound. The ancient sages intuited what modern technology has now demonstrated: the entire Universe is made up of vibration. Both the visible and invisible are simply relative to the sophistication of a being's equipment for "seeing." So it is with the audible and inaudible. Everything that exists has a vibratory signature, a frequency on which it sends and receives. This being true, there are two conclusions: One, by the use of vibration, we can connect with and affect *anything* material. Two, *all* that exists may be a broadcast emanating from a remote place, which can also be reached by vibration. Patterns of sound vibration have been used for thousands of years to align and heal our three bodies. In Sanskrit, this therapy of sound vibration is called *mantra*, which means "delivering us past the limitations of the mind."

The wet tissues of our physical bodies are highly impressionable to the influence of these vibrations. Self-healing through sound vibration is part of the daily practice of all who understand this technology of energy and the mind-body connection. Most people try to gain energy through eating heavy foods, but this overburdens the system and creates blockages. What modern medicine does not yet relate to is the idea that there is more *free* energy available and obtainable at the subtle end of the manifest spectrum. Mantra and vibration avail themselves of vast reserves of free cosmic energy.

Even without mantra, the theory of vibration translates to everyday life. The words we speak shape our minds and bodies, and the sounds coming from our mouths resonate, even attract, certain realities. All sound is a form of mantra, which is why the vibrational quality of what enters into our being is so important. Speaking in a loving and truthful way emits healing vibrations right into our cells, which also vibrate with those feelings.

Sound Vibration Aligns Your Life Force

It was to introduce this idea of vibration and mantra that I previously mentioned the inherent and remarkable programming qualities of the Sanskrit language. This precision is found in the Sanskrit alphabet, which has sixteen vowels, thirty-six consonants, and two special sounds. Every letter is a *phoneme*, or sound unit, which is always pronounced the same way. For this reason, there are no irregularities in the pronunciation of Sanskrit letters or words. Whereas all other languages have varying degrees of irregularities, Sanskrit, which literally means the "perfected language," does not. English, by comparison, is unpredictable, making it difficult for nonnative speakers to learn it. Words such as *there* and *hair* are pronounced the same, as are *home* and *roam*, *blue* and *view*, *see* and *sea*, and so on.

The effects of Sanskrit's perfection are twofold. First, a precise language can be used to make the most precise vibrations. Second, in a perfected language, information and knowledge can be transmitted *over time* without loss or distortion of meaning. For this reason, much of the Vedic wisdom has been passed from generation to generation over thousands of years with almost no change in form or meaning. Sanskrit's precision also allows it to be used to study the effects of sound vibration on our mind/body connection.

Upon hearing the symphony of a great composer, listeners often speak of being transported and transformed by the experience, or even put in a trance. *Trance*, from its Latin root, literally means, "to cross," which happens by the body's listening to and resonance with a given sound or combinations of sound. According to the Vedas, the melodies rearrange the body's atoms and molecules, and energy flows differently within the system. If measured, the body would seem to be producing different chemicals under the impact of the harmonious melodies. With the addition of wise and beautiful words comes the reminder of your greatest self and highest aspirations (*aspiration* meaning "to use the breath"). This is the principle behind the Vedic songs and mantras of eternal truth, sung melodiously.

As in the Old Testament, the much older Vedic texts also say, "In the beginning there was the word." Christians know this word to be *amen*. Muslims know it as *salam*. Jews know it as *shalom*.

The original Sanskrit word, of course, is *om*, which is misspelled. The word is actually spelled *A-U-ung* or ॐ. *A* is the first letter of the Sanskrit alphabet; *U* is a vowel and in the middle, and the last letter is a special letter called *anusvara*, which is the "ung" sound. This is the last letter of the Sanskrit alphabet. A-U-ung refers to the cosmic beginning, middle, and end, the Alpha and the Omega, and everything in between. The om (aum) vibration is the original name of the Supreme Being, the vibratory Avatar, from which all eternity emerges and returns, materially and transcendentally. Om, shalom, amen, salam—the source of everything.

Mystic Letters: Sacred Sounds

With the Sanskrit alphabet, there are deep secrets beyond the precision and stability of the letters. The Sanskrit alphabet is called *Devanagari*, which translates as "the city of the Devas." The Devas, as we have seen, are the Divine beings, helpers of the Avatar, who operate the Laws of Nature (*ritam*). These helpers actually are present in the sound vibration of the fifty-two letters of the alphabet, out of which everything that exists is created. The Vedic version of "in the beginning was the word" means vibration exists before it becomes matter.

The thinkers who framed this system say that while in profound states of meditation, this truth was transmitted or downloaded to them. Other parts of the Vedas were given as teachings left behind by Avatars while visiting Earth. Sanskrit mantras and songs are essential parts of harmonizing the physical, energetic, and mental bodies. The Vedic view, with vibration, follows a logical cause and effect: whatever you listen to, you will think about; whatever you think about, you will speak about; whatever you speak about, you will do; and whatever you do, you will become. For this reason, good listening skills are the inseparable companion to creating healing vibrations of higher consciousness. This is true in the Vedas as surely as it is true in relationships. The Sanskrit for this web of connectedness is *anna*, *prana*, *mana*. In short, what you eat creates your energy and life force, which then becomes your mind. Western science has simply left *prana* out of the equation.

Only in the Vedas are we shown the role that sound vibration plays in aligning our being, our life force, with the Devas and the Laws of Nature. As clearly as communication systems receive signals from distant satellites, the Vedas reveal that a connection is possible and always available to the powerful invisible realities that divinely support and connect all life. The science behind the art of truthful speaking, subtle listening, and mantras that allow us to connect with the Divine Reality is an essential part of the advanced training brought to Earth by the Ultimate Avatars.

The East has been the center of energy science—how our foods create our energy, which creates our minds, and how, in reverse, our thoughts and emotions, the food of our minds, shape our life force and our bodies. Thankfully, the old profit-driven and biased medical paradigm is beginning to give way—as evidenced in the well-documented effects of yoga, chi gong, meditation, and similar energy techniques—giving irrefutable health benefits. Today there are over 100 million yogic practitioners throughout the world—and that number is growing. Plus, with obesity, diabetes, and other such diseases becoming epidemic wherever the modern idea of lifestyle is pursued, healing alternatives have become critical. The body-mind connection demands it. The health of the global community demands it. What the Avatars have said for thousands of years remains true: not only are we what we eat, we are what we say, think, emote, and contemplate. Through the understanding of vibration, it becomes possible to grasp and even witness that we take on the subtle energetic qualities of all that we associate with. Therefore, how we live shapes the quality of our life force.

ḟONORING TḟE ḟEMININE

Namaste, I see you as a sister, mother, daughter, wife, and femine divine.
You are the Shakti, the essence, the heart, and the source of life.
You are in everything, and everything rests on you.
Your laughter is the music of life.

If a culture holds the view that the Divine Reality from which we have all descended is both male and female, then our reincarnation back and forth between male and female bodies takes on new significance. In either, we are in a form that reflects the beauty and secrets of one half of the Divine. We are simultaneously learning about both the terrestrial male and female by having a gender-based body/mind and interacting with the opposite body/mind. In an "I see you as the atma" culture, this can lead to a much more profound and sacred view of the male and female genders.

Although both genders reflect the secrets of Divinity, generally the female wears more of her beauty on the outside, and without being trained to see her as the atma, men around the world have a tendency to be distracted or blinded by her beauty. Being able to see a woman's atma, along with her beauty, is a universal safeguard for both protecting her and balancing the social environment.

With no such vision or safeguard in place, multiple problems have resulted. With unrelenting intensity, the Western world has pushed for female rights but has at the same time gradually come to use female beauty as an inducement to buy products. Her body has become a public (degraded) rather than a private (sacred) vision. Her beauty is used to control and agitate both the male and female mind and to induce consumption literally through addiction. It could be argued that exploitation of the female body as a product has run parallel with the exploitation of the nonrenewable energies of Mother Earth. It may not be a coincidence that the development of the internet has been largely funded by pornography, making access to a degraded vision of her beauty ubiquitous. The great hope of international communication has, in a sense, emerged from the womb of females, but not in a conscious or elegant way.

It is a credit to James Cameron's skill as a filmmaker that, although the Na'vi in *Avatar* are scantily clothed, he managed to create beings with an open, assured, and natural relationship with their bodies. They also exhibit a self-respect and sacred mentality, reflecting the ease of Indigenous cultures' acceptance of their physicality. In the film, Na'vi women are powerful, independent, and respected for skills unique to both their individuality and their gender. If WeQ is intuition and direct perception, it is self-evident that many women come naturally equipped with more of these insightful emotive skills, vital for a sustainable relationship to the Earth. There is also a deep sense of both feminine mystery and her likeness to the All Mother in the film. Traditionally, the Indian culture, exemplified in the two Avatar epics, the *Ramayana* and the *Mahabharata*, felt this connection so deeply that they behaved as if the honor, protection, and empowerment of women were the same as honoring and protecting Mother Bhumi. They saw, as *Avatar* also indicates, the female energy as Mother Nature.

The Sanskrit name for this female energy is *Shakti*. A similar concept appears in Judaism as the female grace of God that descends upon a Jewish household on the evening of the *Shabbat* (the Sabbath on Friday night). In Hebrew she is called the *Shekkinah* and manifests while the woman of the household lights the menorah (the seven sacred candles). Likewise, one of the names of Mother Nature is Shakti Ma— the Mother of all energy. According to the teachings of the Avatars, everything that exists in nature has a male aspect and a female aspect of Shakti, which in reality are never separate. Knowing this, a human male and female do not come together simply for sexual union, for pleasure and/or reproduction, but as an expression of the two fundamental principles of Nature, consciously cooperating with love to make all life possible. Virtually all Indigenous cultures agree that of the two genders, the female energy is the most remarkable and, as the gateway to life, must be given the deepest respect, protection, and understanding.

The Vedas explain that in the beginning of this Universe, the Creator, Brahma, asked the original man and woman, "Who would like to perform the meditation to bring forth life?" The woman volunteered and sat at the center of the circle. Seeing that, the man took a vow that he would protect with his life the circle where the woman sat. Being vulnerable by reproduction, because the woman can more easily be violated and because she is the direct link to the Mother of All, the woman's body is sacred, and all noble men are obliged to protect her rather than exploit her. At its most severe, rape is a weapon of war. What is done to women is also done to Mother Earth. The female is directly connected to Her heart and so acts to protect all life whenever possible.

As Above, So Below

The Vedas tell us repeatedly that the male and female forms that we see all around us—and that are also embodied within each of us—

are literally made in the "image of the original Supreme Male and Female Beings." The original Male and Female Supreme Beings are the prototype—a Mr. and Mrs. Divine—who live for eternity in the Transcendental realm (and that's a long time!). All this does *not*, however, mean that Male and Female Divines are two different Beings—they are not. You might want to read that last sentence again. This is a great secret of the Avatars. They are *two* aspects of the *same* Being—and, according to the Vedas, are eternally in love and never tiring of the other's company. Inconceivably, simultaneously, one *and* two.

These Male Divine and Female Divine forms are replicated in all that is created from them, just as when humans make a baby, that child has genetic material from both parents. It is a step-down kind of process into matter. As the original emanations of the Supreme Male and Female forms enter matter at the highest level, they become Mother and Father Nature. In this role, one of them now is an extender (Father Nature) and one a receiver (Mother Nature). At the cosmic level, the Veda says, there is a mother who is the sum total of all matter. This means that all the countless Universes are part of Her body.

As we descend further down the scale of creation, a single Universe is also an organism with a Mother Nature and a Father Nature intertwined, embraced, and dancing, if you will—cosmic genetic material unfolding. A Universe is the result of Father and Mother Nature embracing and remaining intertwined.

All of nature is also held together by the union of "male and female" bonds. Modern science describes this as positive and negative or electrons and protons, but in the visioning of ancient wisdom, Nature is not impersonal—She is intensely personal. The Sun, for example, is considered male, and the Sunshine female. Together, they comprise our experience of the Sun. Just as we say married human couples are "one flesh," so the Sun and the Sunshine are "married"—

a sort of Mr. and Mrs. Sun. Another example is the rose and its fragrance. The structure of the rose is masculine, and its scent is the Shakti; together they are the rose. If the two divorce, there is no rose. If the Sun and Sunshine divorce, there is no life.

Finally, continuing the descent, planets are also Mothers with "families" of amazing entities living on their bodies. This is Earth or Mata Bhumi. And stepping down even further—and even though the atma is neither female nor male—our bodies as mothers, fathers, and children are the sacred containers made from the descending emanations of the original Male and Female Supreme Beings.

As we learn to see all beings as divine, this Avatar lesson is meant to deepen that process for you. In properly understanding and honoring the female, our intention and attention should start at the *highest level* of creation within matter. When we namaste—"I see the real you"—we can now be aware that we are not only saying, "I see you as the atma," but also, "I see your atma shining *and* your *body* as the sacred image of the Transcendental Divine." This practice creates a deep reverence for the female (and also the male) and helps displace our tendency to objectify her endless beauty due to our lack of understanding.

Starhawk, a teacher in the Celtic and Pagan traditions, put it this way: "The Goddess does not rule the world. She is the world. Manifest in each of us, She can be known internally by every individual, in all Her magnificent diversity."

On Earth, we all understand the woman is the giver of life, the gateway of birth (a true sacrifice). This genius of the woman to profoundly create in countless ways is evident to most anyone watching: the woman is—like the Earth—the endless giver and worthy of the greatest honor, love, and protection. When this fails, the Avatars start to make plans.

Each female, then, is the Shakti of some aspect of the All Mother. In one sense, she contains all aspects of Mother Nature, but she is also empowered in specific ways. This is also largely true for a culture. The women of a culture are its Shakti—the repository of all the customs and subtle nuances of the society. They are the librarians and the libraries at the same time. This is why "Miss Manners" is never "Mr. Manners." The Shakti is our reliable and ever-present guide to our ancestors and holds them in Her womb, not only to produce another being but as a continuation of the history and legacy of the ancestors of Her culture. For this reason, conquering or neighboring kings often attempted strategic alliances with other countries by marrying those countries' princesses. This was not for passion—as kings by their power and wealth could already have as much sex as they desired. The princesses were to be their "Miss Manners"—not only to extend their power, but to guide them in socially and politically correct behaviors.

This Wisdom Female, who is central to the plot of the *Ramayana* and the *Mahabharata*, is the missing priestess in our current global culture. Her presence in Mr. Cameron's film *Avatar* was another brilliant and timely reminder of what we have forgotten.

When the representative of Mother Earth Herself is not consulted, heard, honored, and deferred to in our councils and assemblies, we who represent the original voice of Bhumi are concerned, sad, and offended. It is the Shakti, after all, who must be honored and protected if we are to sustain human life with compassion and integrity.

In *Avatar*, both the Male and Female are leaders, each with unique powers and dignity. They cooperate for the good of each other and of all. In order for this to take place in our world, we must first tell a story of the beauty and value of each gender. They must be equally valued for their empowerments and skills. For men—for the warrior—this means that their physical strength should be dedicated to the protection of all who are innocent, as well as women, children, and the elderly, from all cultures. This is, to give another culture's example, the Way of the Samurai. No enemy is ever a woman, child, or elder. This has been the ethos of the best Indigenous cultures. In India, the great epics—the Avatar stories—are both about the descent of the Divine Being to fight the ignorance and evil that threatens Mother Earth, demeans the female, and leaves vulnerable those who are innocent.

Just as thousands of years ago the spiritual and intuitive arts reached a high level of perfection in India and other cultures, so our technological phase of evolutionary development today has reached its pivotal moment. We have weapons of mass destruction that can destroy all life in a moment, yet we dare not use them. Simultaneously, we are tampering with aspects of the genetic basis of all life, putting our future in the hands of profit-only scientists and corporations. Notwithstanding the present-day debasement of the female as a product in the media, and under the heel of fundamentalist religion, another and very hopeful development has been evolving over the last hundred years. A significant proportion of the world has internet and cell-phone access with friends, colleagues, and lovers in every nation. Films like *Avatar* are now box-office hits around the globe. In the midst of the IQ crisis, and despite the horrific treatment of women in many places around the globe, millions of women in many countries are standing up and into a new kind of power, influence, and freedom.

The yoga movement is an example of this transformation. Unlike coercive or proselytizing religions with billion-dollar budgets for converting the pagans, Yoga has spread quietly and without the use of force, budget, or fanfare. Yoga and the Vedic view from which it emerged stands by definition against promotion by force, let alone by demanding a monaural religious conclusion. Yoga demands no earthly intermediary. In its myriad forms, it begins directly with our bodies and how we live on Earth. It encourages a platform of healthy eating and living as a vegetarian or as low on the food chain as possible. At its simplest, through the very *asanas* (poses) that are done across the globe by millions every morning, Yoga seeks our balance, harmony, and cooperation with Nature and one another. It encourages so-called moral values—restraints and observances to maximize both health and peaceful interaction—ideas generally valued by all religions at their best. Yoga's creed, if it has one, suggests that we discover our true nature and live accordingly; that we consciously do the least possible harm to all beings, called *ahimsa* in Sanskrit; and that we teach by personal example rather than by spouting platitudes. To quote a modern-day yogi, Mahatma Gandhi, speaking the wisdom of the Avatars, "Be the change you wish to see in the world." Yoga discourages the use of intoxicants and harmful foods. Yoga advises that sexuality should be healthy, full of integrity, consensual, and sacred—and again, should cause no harm. And Yoga supports yet never demands worship in many forms, including those promoted by the many faiths across the world, as well as the many Vedic paths.

It is estimated today that at least 80 percent of the Yoga practitioners worldwide are female. Globally, there are some thirty million Indians living outside of India. Yet inside India, both now and in the past, one does not see millions of females practicing physical yoga, which has been a traditionally male practice. To the yogi, this asks an interesting question: is it possible that the millions of female yogis who are quietly changing the world by the practice of Yoga, by the way they spend their money, by seeking a balanced life in an unbalanced world, were all male yogis in India in a previous life? Perhaps they are the vital helper cells in Mother Earth's immune system. The underlying viewpoint, perhaps unspoken or even unconscious to many—but self-evident by their desire to practice Yoga—is that we must find a more balanced, more flexible, healthier, and less destructive way to live on Mata Bhumi. This is also the message of the Avatars, who by definition have descended, and always descend to bring the world back to balance. The female, in her present-day power, in her developing WeQ intelligence, is now talking to the male IQ intelligence about a new kind of relationship, mediated by 3rd IQ perception and supported by both Father and Mother Nature.

Bowing to the Wisdom

In the animal world, the female bird is clearly in charge of the nest. Our own intelligence should tell us that the being made to carry babies, protect them, and feed them would also have a built-in intelligence for the preservation of all life. Of course women have this. And as we consider the environment today, at countless cultures, it is also strikingly obvious that the genius of that life-affirming voice is not being sufficiently listened to. We are at a historical moment that clearly tells us, if we're listening, to honor the feminine, protect her gift, and ask her to please speak more. For women, this should not be one more task on an already impossibly long list. It should simply be part of our learning to listen. To say, "I see you—the giver of life, bounty, beauty."

In the Vedas, the maintainer of all is called Vishnu, and his Shakti (the female energy), his female accomplice, is Lakshmi—also known in English as Lady Luck (from *lak*). This suggests that the ancient secret is to let the maker of life decide how we live, what we eat, and even how money should be spent. Over and over again it is evident that men, when under pressure or disempowered, actually waste money. Microfinancing groups give about 85 percent of their funds to women for this reason: women under pressure are better with money.

Every day, individually, we can make a conscious effort to hear from the female about how to live on our planet. This is a start. It's no coincidence Mother Earth is female. Would it be a surprise that the All Mother speaks more easily through women? Of course not. In a balanced world, compassion and concern for the good of all occur more naturally in women. Exceptions excepted. The Avatar teaching is that we should listen very carefully to the wisdom voice coming from the Sacred Feminine. At this most crucial hour, this is the descent, this is the return of the Great Mother.

SIX

FROM CORPORATION
TO COOPERATION

Namaste, I see your strength protecting and providing for all.
You inspire us when your tender care for all life informs your global visions.
As strong as a thunderbolt but soft as a rose, you harvest
and steward the gifts of prosperity.

Every culture in varying degrees has noble qualities. Each culture's views and practices have been shaped by the climate, topography, rivers, and arable land of the geographic area in which the culture has arisen. Although India is at present fragmented in many ways, it is the ancient home of the profound Vedic wisdom and teachings of the Ultimate Avatars, which remain vibrantly alive there. Those teachings were given as Universal empowerments and deep knowledge for all humans, not just for India. What matters is Universal truth, across cultures, and whether that truth can help the world come back to balance. To teach Universal truth, language is an essential tool.

The paradox of language, however, is that it can be used to both reveal and obscure the truth. To speak from the Avatars' point of view about the dilemma and potential of modern-day corporations, a few Sanskrit words and their meanings need to be introduced.

In earlier chapters, we talked about the invisible laws of Mother Nature (for example, gravity), which are called the ritam. Related to this word, etymologically, is a word more well-known in the West: *karma*—meaning "inevitable cause and effect." Karma is no more complicated than that—except that it includes *all* cause and effect, including the moral consequences of our actions and thoughts, which science rarely includes in its cause-and-effect equation. Ironically, the modern scientific idea that every action has an equal and opposite reaction was first described in the Vedic texts. Our English word *creativity* also comes from this word, the *kri* root of karma.

A third and vital word, also related etymologically, is *dharma*, from *dhri*, which translates as "the essential nature of something, which, if that essential nature is taken away, that thing is no longer itself." For example, if the liquidity is removed from water, it is no longer water. To understand the depth of the idea, one could also say that if the creativity were taken out of William Shakespeare—his essential nature—he would no longer be Shakespeare.

Dharma can also mean the essential nature of a country, or a system, or a farm, or an individual atma, and that should be the most balanced way that it can cause the least damage and act for the most good of all. Once you know your dharma, your duties rest on that knowledge.

Talking with the Angels (Devas)

The important difference between the animal kingdom (who instinctively follow their dharma), the Devas (or divine helpers as the Laws of Nature personified), and humans is that *only* humans can go profoundly against the Laws of Nature. The Devas are both the Laws of Nature and the enforcers of those laws. Animals by design and instinct are forced to and almost invariably follow their natures. When we say, "It's a dog's life," nobody is confused by what kind of life that likely is—least of all the dog. Only we humans can use our free will to oppose Mother Nature.

In the teachings of the Avatars, the campus—this matrix of incontrovertible natural laws—is not random. The University is not an accident, and all our actions and thoughts have consequences at some future time. Our having freedom does not mean we are exempt from the reactions that arise from violating the campus rules—rules no more arbitrary than the laws of physics. Given this truth, to follow and to listen to the universal code of behaviors for humans that conforms to the Laws of Nature is to act on behalf of the good of all. This is dharma, this is truth.

Breaking the Rules

In *Avatar*, the visitors to the planet Pandora, with their mercenary army in tow, were a mining operation of the worst kind, "from a dying planet." The parallels with current-day Afghanistan and Iraq, or any other place where exploitation usurps human rights and disturbs environmental balance, are obvious. The ultimately futile conclusion of such damaging endeavors is nicely summarized in the name of the mineral they are seeking: *Unobtanium*. Perhaps Mr. Cameron is pointing to the ancient Vedic concept of *Maya*, which refers to the world of matter as a mirage we are chasing in the desert of space but where permanent happiness cannot be obtained. Isn't material happiness a kind of *Unobtanium*? Therefore, the Vedas remind us, we should not destroy Nature for our pleasures, temporary or long-term.

A large corporation, with a CEO running it, no matter his or her intentions, is limited in what it can do for "the good of all." A corporation's legal obligations are foremost to maximize profit for the shareholders, to pay taxes and, finally, to work within or around the laws of a given country. If either of the latter two points is excessively confining, those running a corporation will often decide to move to a place where taxes and laws are less restrictive. This is challenging. In the modern corporate world, there is no clear guideline on how to do business in a way that balances profit with a concerted effort on behalf of the good of all—meaning workers' conditions and wages, the community's positive growth, and the environment's health.

In spite of no guidelines, there are still amazing and visionary CEOs who do a great deal to find this balance, but it's not easy. In *Avatar*, James Cameron uses a foreign planet as the location, but he was clearly trying to show the most rapacious side of the corporate model. It speaks volumes that many of us probably saw that as a fairly standard model. The human rights and environmental records of resource-extracting corporations have all too often been abysmal and disheartening. And the unelected corporate hierarchy having excessive power and control over our government, while operating inside our democracy, is a constant irony that threatens our modern political system. There is a surprising amount of support for corporations whose bottom line is only profit, with no thought for what might be called the common good. Resolving this tension between exploitation and cooperation is one of the next evolutionary needs of our modern world. The ancient Avatars spoke of this as one of the key issues of living honorably on Mother Earth.

In a 1970s *New York Times Magazine* article, the famous economist Milton Friedman put it like this: "There is one and only one social responsibility of business—to use its resources and engage in activities designed to increase its profits so long as it stays within the rules of the game, which is to say, engages in open and free competition without deception or fraud."

With profit as the driving force of business, and deception and fraud even harder to control in Third World countries, we need to take a deeper look at the Indigenous worldview as a universal source of values to help keep the planet's dharma in balance.

Making History

It's important to understand how contrary the profit motive is to most Indigenous cultures, not to mention their relationship to resources. The Indigenous worldview inherently says no one can truly own the Earth's resources—they belong to the Great Mother and the land is sacred. Part of a speech attributed to Chief Seattle in the land rush of the 1800s still applies today: "How can you buy or sell the sky—the warmth of the land? The idea is strange to us. Yet we do not own the freshness of the air or the sparkle of the water."

Still, one could imagine a sort of prototypical corporate structure in the long-ago tribal hunting parties that worked together to hunt game. The CEO was the hunting-party chief, the salesmen were the hunters, the marketing department would have made the arrows, and the accounting department would divide the kill. What could be more human than to make a profit (find and collect enough food) that allows survival of a community? Even seemingly harmless small corporations or small businesses are like this. They are the benign hunting and food-gathering groups, though due to technology their environmental impact may still be damaging.

Incorporating Wisdom

From the viewpoint of the Avatars and the perspective of the Earth Mother, there are no people or creatures on planet Bhumi who are not precious, unique, and deserving of a dignified life. Creating slaves or wiping out species, oceans, and forests and decimating a citizenry to fill the pockets of a few are contrary to dharma, religion, and truth. Anyone with feeling can see that Mother Earth, or the All Mother, cannot be happy with this sad state of affairs. Everything we extract from Mother Earth comes out at some hard-to-quantify yet undeniable ecological price.

The solution does not lie either in governmental regulations or unregulated entrepreneurial fervor. World poverty today is the result of a schism, a lack of relationship and consciousness, that is found in both our institutions and our own minds. We need a percentage of land kept in trust as the common area for all, and we need a way to extract reasonable resources, but the irresponsible use of the powers of technology have amplified the negative ways we attempt this.

The Avatar wisdom says that wise and dharmic leaders are the real solution, along with an ethos of cooperation. Our IQ and WeQ minds need to wake up to a level of consciousness that accepts our differences and uses one another's strengths, creates greater cooperation, and learns how to hold a bigger vision of our relation to one another and to all life—to see our inherent unification. Dharmic enterprises with Universal values that hold themselves accountable for the good of all, while earning a reasonable profit, need to become our new corporate models. As spiritual aspirants, our goal should always be to bring our lives to balance, back to their dharma. Echoing the teachings of the Avatar over five thousand years later, Marian Wright Edelman, the founder of the Children's Defense Fund, wrote, "Be strong and courageous and leave the results to God.... Don't be afraid to be a voice in the wilderness for children and the poor. It's the moral and sensible thing to do."

So, yes, there are some answers and there is always room for relentless optimism. According to the Vedas, there are no complete cures while in the material world. But still, it is necessary that we strive for increased balance and harmony.

The Good, the Bad, and the Hopeful

Guiding us along a spectrum from light to dark, the Vedas speak of one kind of human who chooses to profit no matter what the cost of suffering to the many and another kind of human who feels the pain of all beings and thus works for the most sustainable life possible—for the good of all. Those souls who simply harm others for their own selfish gains are called Asuras and their behavior is described as *tamasic*, meaning "lost in ignorance." These are the students in the University who are ignoring the great wisdom teachings and purposefully or unconsciously destroying the campus. The Avatar always descends from the higher realm to stop them.

Those humans who live and work with compassion and in balance with the ritam, the Laws of Mother Nature, are called *sattvic*, meaning, "in harmony with the ritam [Bhumi laws] and Devas." One group is enlightened, and the other is "endarkened." The Vedic culture always hopes that students choose to "work in the light," supporting dharma as much as possible. Most humans are somewhere between the tamasic and the sattvic in a third category of beings who are often forgetful, self-absorbed, or ego driven. This third group is called *rajasic*. Their selfish attitudes cause problems and imbalances even though that may not be their intention. The more humans who cultivate a sattvic lifestyle, the better—for us and for the environment. This sattvic way of being is one of the main teachings in the two great epics, the *Ramayana* and the *Mahabharata*. It leads to reasonable ownership and consumption and is based in cooperation.

Casting Call—The Dharma of Societies

So if the very nature of the Vedic culture is to support dharma and seek balance for the good of all, you might be thinking: *Then why did India eventually produce the caste system of class by birth?*

The history is remarkably complex, but there is one main answer to the question. India's original teaching—the Vedas—promoted what is more accurately a class system based on inherent skill or talent. While children were young, or in school, the elders observed their behaviors and abilities. It became clear that most people fell into one of four work (or skill) categories according to their nature, *Brahmins*, *Kshatrias*, *Vaishyas*, and *Shudras*.

One group was predominantly thinkers—intellectuals, scientists, spiritual leaders—in other words, those whose work demanded thought, patience, nonviolence, and the ability to retain knowledge. A person with these skills was called a *Brahmin*.

A second group was seen to be predominantly fearless, powerful, courageous, tolerant of pain, and action oriented, and to be natural leaders. Those in this group were trained to be warriors, protectors, and administrators. They were called *Kshatrias*.

The third group was predominantly inclined to produce wealth, food, and other valuables. These people had entrepreneurial natures. They were called *Vaishyas*.

The fourth group were made of *Shudras*, those who predominantly had an inclination toward service or who were craftsmen, artisans, and skilled and unskilled laborers. By following their tendency toward service, they held society together for the improved benefit of all. It takes inherent humility, stamina, and courage to perform jobs that must be done but that so few wish to do or are even capable of doing.

In the Vedas, these four groups are described as part of the whole social body. The thinkers are the head, the protectors are the arms, the providers are the belly, and the serving class are the feet. Each group is considered vital, just as any sane person values his or her head, arms, belly, and feet as amazing and vital. This is the nature of the original so-called caste system: four classes of people doing work that is in accordance with their inherent abilities. In a less complex world, these four groups would be obvious and natural and be viewed simply as each one's particular dharma. One's dharma, or essential nature, is called one's *sva-dharma*. Today, we would call this someone's natural ability. Acting according to our nature creates less friction in the social body and leads to cooperation.

We all immediately understand the agony that is caused by forcing a child or young adult to become, say, a lawyer, doctor, or engineer when the person really wants to be, and his or her inherent nature is to be, an artist or musician. It is painful for an artist to be forced to be a lawyer, or vice versa, because the person would then be out of balance with his or her sva-dharma—his or her own true nature.

For each occupational dharma, there is a set of rules and duties that governs conduct, just as we have professional codes for modern occupations. The police and soldiers are known for their code of conduct. So it is with teachers, doctors, craftsman, or any profession.

This intelligent method of determining career by ability rather than by birth is the original Vedic social system. Assigning caste by birth is a subversion of this search for people's best abilities. It should be self-evident that being the son or daughter of a professor—a Brahmin—does not ensure the child will have intellectual abilities. To force an occupation upon someone by circumstances of birth is a perversion of the original Vedic practice. To know one's true sva-dharma is one of the grand keys to a fulfilling, balanced, productive life—the possibility of living according to one's own nature.

Bhumi Dharma—Our Responsibility to Mother Earth

From a dharmic perspective, our modern democracies are largely run by unelected institutions in a cash-based social system. This is not casteism, it is "cash-tism." Those with money are the new global Western royalty, regardless of the dharma (or lack of it) behind how that money was obtained, who was harmed, or what was destroyed.

We have not yet found a modern, global dharma that describes and ensures that our corporate actions will result in the optimum benefit for the most people. And this has nothing to do with socialism. This has to do with compassion and the possibility of having visionary thinkers in leadership roles who understand their sva-dharma and our collective Bhumi dharma, our responsibility to Mother Earth. This can only happen in a culture where each occupation has a true code of honor and conduct that is not corruptible by money. We are all in this together as children living off the selfless gifts of the All Mother.

We need to regain the truth of the trees and their tree-uth. That truth is real wealth. Today money is no longer a promissory note for real wealth but is a largely degraded promise—the Great Lie—that says that when all of the *Unobtanium* is finally extracted, everything still will be fine.

We need less casteism, less clash-ism, less classism, less cash-tism, and *more* dharma. We need Bhumi dharma, millions of atmas seeing the endless generosity of Mother Earth and the divinity of one another, working together to reweave the web of Nature. We need a new kind of CEO. We need a CCO—a Chief Conscience Officer—who reviews the corporation's relationship to all aspects of society and to the generous, resilient love of Mother Nature. This would support us all to make certain there is a heart beating in the chest of the corporate warrior. This is the Hope of Pandora's Box. This is the teaching of the Avatar. We must see it in ourselves. We must be it in ourselves. We must envision it in one another.

TWICE BORN AND
RITES OF PASSAGE

*Namaste, I see you on a great journey, holding within you the wisdom and
creativity of all places and cultures and many lifetimes of learning.
You are a brave traveler, rising again and again
to the next challenge of life.*

Maintaining a namaste view in the midst of a busy, often crazy, and even violent world requires steady practice. It is hard enough to see a friend or loved one this way. It is even more challenging to see the atma in someone opposed to you or trying to harm you. At the same time, seeing all beings as atmas is in no way meant to induce passivity or short out the necessary defensive responses needed to counter those who are causing harm. The fact that all beings are atmas on the campus does not excuse their ignorant or destructive actions. The school bully—in all its forms—still has to be dealt with by someone.

Our everyday experience is that most people are forgetful of their Divine nature. Here, just as in material colleges, only a few people are working on their PhDs (that is, seeing all beings as divine), while the majority of students are in lower grades not yet ready to see everyone in a divine way. In India, this namaste greeting shows that trying to see the atma in everyone is a national pastime. Nevertheless, without the right awareness, even such a gesture becomes an empty ritual and simply means hello.

Since the atma goes from body to body over many lifetimes, each birth as a human includes not only the accumulated learning from past lives, but also a record of what and to whom karmic obligations are owed from actions and agreements in those previous lives.

Dream the Body Electric

According to the Vedas, all human beings have three bodies: one is their atma or spiritual body, whose consciousness powers the next two material bodies. Like a nut with a covering and a shell, this spiritual body lies at the core of all beings. The second body is called the subtle body or mental body. It is also called our dream body. When we dream at night or even daydream, we are traveling outside the physical body in a dream body. The most dense and obvious covering is our third body, the physical body. Like our clothing, which comes and goes, our dense physical body is the furthest from our true self. That is one of the essential messages of the Avatars: we are not our physical or our dream bodies.

Dreaming is a kind of out-of-body experience from which we see and feel experiences that seem in the moment as real as physical experiences. Watching a film is a variation on the dream-body experience. Before there were movies and video technology, there were the Vedas and similar stories in other cultures by which the elders showed us the visions of who we are. Songs with words and music have a similar effect. They project visions onto the screens of our minds, attuning us to a remote experience. These auditory and visual technologies have been used by elders of Indigenous cultures since the beginning of time to teach and present images to young minds.

The film *Avatar* is connected to this conversation about out-of-body experiences. It mirrors the Veda's philosophical analysis of how we go from one body to another on our journey of learning who we really are—and who we really are not. From this perspective, there is no such thing as death. The Avatars teach us over and over: dying is only a shedding of skin, removing a shirt—it's like watching your body as a car being towed away. We even see this change in our own lives, from baby to child to adult to elder. It is at the time of death in our subtle or physical body that we are taken to the place where our next physical body is generated as the result of previous actions and desires. We are born repeatedly in new vehicles that we have "purchased" with our previous actions.

Put another way, when a baby is born, on the outside its fresh new body is a blank disc waiting for new impressions. On the inside, volumes of learning and experience are stored from hundreds of previous human lives. Inside both the physical body and the subtle body is the atma, or spiritual body. We never really know who the new baby was in a previous life: a king or queen, a saint, your mother or father, your enemy, or a complete stranger—perhaps a prodigy.

In cultures where this view of continuity from birth to birth exists, the elders perform conscious-awakening rituals for the newly arrived atma, guiding the unfoldment of its being into maturity. To this day, the elders of India understand and practice the sixteen *Samskaras*, meaning "refinements," "perfections," or rites of passage, for all children. Even in the absence of a clear view that the atma is a visiting Transcendental Being, the organic, cyclic view of life led all Indigenous peoples to treat the developing human with specific and appropriate rituals to empower and guide them—literally, rites of passage—at each stage of development. The similarity to plants and trees is clear. Gardeners understand that from seedling to maturity, precise actions help the plant to reach full potential. All of these teachings are part of the dharma of being an elder and parent. Even without considering or accepting the concept of the atma, an aware parent with good instincts will understand the importance of honoring the stages of the unfolding of a baby into young adulthood. Five thousand years ago, the Avatar Krishna, warned of society's becoming fragmented if our dharmas were not maintained and children were not taken care of. No evolved Indigenous person could relate to people who have children and then do not take an active part in raising them. To do so would be an extreme violation of the ritam and the dharma of marriage and parenting.

In *Avatar*, James Cameron powerfully constructed the transformation of Jake Sully, who starts in the film as an "empty jarhead with no knowledge and a good brain." He is paraplegic; the loss of function in his legs is clearly a metaphor for humans slowly losing their connection with Mother Earth because it is assumed he lost his legs fighting to extract natural resources for state and corporate interests. Jake ends up spending six years out in space because his own culture would not give him back his legs and "there was nothing better to do in his meaningless life." In Zen Buddhism, there is a famous story of a PhD visiting a Zen master, who greets the professor by brewing tea. He pours until the tea overflows into the saucer and then all over the table. At this point the professor shouts, "Can't you see the cup is full?" The Master replies, "Yes, I can, and if you don't empty it, I won't be able to teach you anything."

Wild to Be Born

Those of us who have gone to gurus and elders from India and other ancient teaching lineages know this moment very well. Speaking personally, I can tell you that being raised without rites of passage and as "an empty jarhead with a good brain," combined with the sincere desire to learn, made me an ideal candidate to be "reborn." In India, the Sanskrit word for reborn or "twice born" is *dwija. Dwi* means "distinct or second," and *ja* means "birth," *ja* being the same root as *gen* in the

English word *genetics*. In spite of good intentions, parents often have limited understanding of prenatal care, natural birth, breastfeeding, the effects of bottled homogenized milk and processed solid food, along with no awareness of what is best for a particular body type. Most school curriculums are not tailored to the student, and sexual awakening is haphazard and without reference to the Sacred Male and Female Divines. There is very little or no training and preparation for marriage and childcare and, finally, in the moment most crucial to all—death—we mostly see confusion, drama, and fear.

In *Avatar*, Jake Sully is thought by the Na'vi to be "like a child, a moron with no common sense." But through his willingness to listen in the deepest possible way—as much as could be shown in a film— Jake is transformed into a respected member of their culture and qualified "to speak."

The elders of India have a similar way of explaining this rebirthing process. Think of matter around us as a matrix of material life. This entire matrix is the body of the Great Mother. To Her, every part of nature, of the material world, is conscious. In contrast, for smaller beings like ourselves, our consciousness pervades only our own bodies and minds. For this reason, matter can cover us with its unconscious and inert nature, causing us to forget who we really are.

The Sanskrit word for matter is *gu*, curiously similar to our English word *goo*, a sticky substance in which one can get stuck. When we are born, we come in covered by goo, unconscious of who we are— the atma. The atma is completely submerged in the physicality of bodily development. This is natural and unavoidable. I once saw a T-shirt for babies that said, "I pee, I poo, I drink my moo. I'm a baby, that's what I do." According to the Vedas, we have all been there many times. During this physical stage of evolution, we are encompassed by what is called in Sanskrit *ahamkara*, or the ego shell. Ahamkara means, "I am matter—I am the goo." In short, we have completely forgotten who we are. In our young developmental stage, this ego shell acts as a protective covering. Interestingly, the word dwija—twice born—also means "egg born" like a bird, which is actually born twice, the first time with a shell and the second time by breaking that shell, the ego shell, thereby giving birth to the true self. According to the teachings of the Avatar, this process of rebirthing all persons as atmas is an important safeguard against the dangers of excessive ego conflict in society.

The ego-shell stage is similar to using training wheels on a bicycle. The shell protects us but it also keeps us from seeing and hearing things as they truly are. And like the training wheels, the shell needs to come off at a certain age, but it cannot come off by itself. The problem with a predominately IQ-based education is that it can exacerbate and thicken the mental ego shell to the point where it is as impenetrable as the physical ego shell. Then there are two hard shells covering one unawakened atma. The Avatar teachings would say that scientists are often limited by this ego shell causing them to use their brilliance to dominate Mother Nature instead of cooperate with Her. In Jake's case, his lack of an IQ education was an advantage in his Indigenous rebirthing.

Adult Education: The Question of Dharma

Before India was colonized and its original educational system was still intact, the timing of this twice-born process was built into both rites of passage and a second-birth process. Through a variety of ancient meditations and a guided curriculum, students were gradually made aware of their true natures as atmas. Schools were generally run by a husband-and-wife team and were known as *gurukulas* that taught IQ, WeQ, and 3rd IQ learning, culminating in the necessary skills for the profession best suited to the individual's nature. The word *guru* in gurukula is often mistakenly thought of as a charismatic cult leader wearing flowing robes with total control over his followers. There are a few of those, but *guru* actually means *gu*, as in "goo," and *ru*, meaning "remover." So a guru is a wise elder who helps us to replace an ego-only concept of self, such as the material mind and body (they are literally the remover of the goo), with the greater conception that we are all eternal atmas evolving in a grand universal process. One who has been initiated into this understanding by a guru is considered twice born. This process helps the initiate see all living beings as fellow students (namaste) who are divine visitors from the Transcendental realm, here to learn by gathering experiences and, eventually, to graduate. Along with this teaching is the understanding that the protection and preservation of Mata Bhumi, Mother Earth, must be considered in all our actions.

If and when we grasp this subtle understanding of who we are, our dharma, or tree-uth, is then acted out in three ways, which present themselves as the key questions of human life.

As previously mentioned, the first is Bhumi dharma, or "What do I owe the Earth?" According to the Avatar teachings, because we are here, taking up space, learning and using the campus resources, the obligation to our Mother is to restore and maintain Her body as perfectly as possible for all Her other atmas. In short, we all owe Mother Earth the respect of cleaning up our own messes before we leave. It is just a matter of being respectful to Father and Mother Nature. After all, they feed us, clothe us, and give us all the resources we need. The least we can do is show our gratitude by restoring what we have used.

The second dharma is sva-dharma, or "How can I be true to myself in this body?" This dharma requires that we understand and act in accordance with the nature of the body/mind we have acquired in this lifetime. As far as possible, we should try to find a career that is suited to our physical and mental natures. To do so will lead to physical and mental happiness. Just as a station wagon or a sports car is designed to perform a function, so is our body/mind best suited for a particular kind of work. We should not let either cast-ism or cash-tism force us into the wrong occupation. For our spiritual progress and for our physical and mental health, we have the right, and with it the struggle, to be our true selves.

The third and final dharma question is, "Who am I in eternity, and how do I recover my Transcendental nature, even in the midst of the stress and chaos of material life?" Transcendental, remember, means that part of each of us is not from here, and that part is who we really are for eternity, not just this lifetime. In this dharma we are not humans having a spiritual experience; we are atmas having a material experience. Knowing who you are in eternity is called *sanatan* dharma—or remembering your true Transcendental eternal nature. Through the helpful rites of our transition from one stage of life to another and through the awakening that occurs in our second birth, we are able to cooperate better with Mother Earth, be our truest selves in our bodies, and remain mindful of our eternal natures and highest purposes here.

A culture with a system of cradle-to-grave rites of passage uses its wise elders to keep the process of life integrated. We are organic beings whose finite experience of life unfolds in successive stages. Knowing how to work harmoniously with these cyclic changes that occur over time is the indicator that we are listening to Mother Nature and the Devas.

In the absence of rituals of the twice born and rites of passage, we risk having a society of individuals who are confused about the meaning of their current stage of unfoldment. Ignoring rites of passage, we have substituted in a culture of "perpetual youth" instead of celebrating the natural stages of life's development. It is true that the atma is eternally young, but it is equally true that while we live in physical bodies, we need to honor the evolutionary stages of life.

EIGHT

The ancestors and elders

*Namaste, I see you becoming a wise elder, telling ancient stories,
patiently speaking the truth, leading the children on vision quests.
You are the roots of our tree, and in your kind eyes the lamp
of inspiration touches the next generation.*

had Isaac Newton written about some of our wireless transmission products—cell phones, the internet, even television—a few hundred years ago, he would have been declared a superstitious fool peddling questionable science about how the world really works. Today, wireless devices are ubiquitous. Remarkably, machines smaller than pocket-size can, in an instant, download and display text, sound, and images and even stream video. With great genius, the IQ scientists have demonstrated what WeQ thinkers have always known: that the Universe, all of Mother Nature (and even beyond), is by its very nature always in a state of sending and receiving wireless signals. People do it, birds do it, plants and animals do it—I guess scientists can do it now, too. If our scientists can do it, then why wouldn't the Supreme Intelligence be able to do something similar, albeit infinitely more complex? Indeed, scientists have learned this because it is the nature of intelligence.

Calling Long Distance

Just as our planet is currently encircled by innumerable channels and frequencies containing mega amounts of information, the Universe itself conducts its affairs by means of wireless communication. Our ancient ancestors understood that humans have a built-in sending and receiving device that requires only activation. We now have cell phones, but our own cells have always been a kind of phone, capable of sending and receiving countless types of signals and transmissions. Humans created the internet as a vibratory repository of our cultural communications, and nature has always had an "inner net" from which humans could learn by receiving "downloads." The "technology" required to connect is called Yoga, which is the art and science of linking with some wireless reality, culminating in connecting to our Original Source.

Elders who have been "plugged in" all their lives act as tech support and as the hard drive or storage device for the living wisdom of a culture. According to the Avatar, even having the downloaded words on hard copy is no substitute for receiving the live transmission from an enlightened human being.

In the Jewish mystical path of the Kabballah, the Hebrew language is written without vowels and uses only consonants. To learn to pronounce the words correctly, the words have to be whispered into the ear of a student by an elder. The Kabballistic saying is, "In the Torah, there are two kinds of letters, the white and the black. However, the black letters cannot be understood without first seeing the white letters."

Historically, ancient cultures have purposely passed their truths on using specially trained elders. As the tree-uth passes through them, they are acting as the roots of the Home Tree and the Tree of Ancestors. The intelligent question is therefore: How do we continue to hear the deepest wisdom of our ancestors?

Wanted: Wise Elders

Under the impact of massive changes and as a byproduct of exponential technological growth, our modern world has not developed sacred rites of passage or anything like a second-birth process. Electricity and lights—obviously great discoveries—have nonetheless distorted our connection with the natural cycles, daily, weekly, monthly, annually, and from the beginning to the end of our lives. How many people today know which phase of the moon we're in on any given day? Television has replaced the ancestral fire and is motivated by commercial desires instead of the sharing of Universal Wisdom. From childhood, we are literally trained to be consumers. It has been said that by the time the average North American is sixty years old, he will have watched fifteen years of television and hundreds of thousands of commercials, and I'm sure this is becoming a global statistic. Just as our ever-expanding landfills continue to overflow with countless obsolete and disposable products that once seemed vital, so our elders are now consigned to an "old folk's home" to wait out their last days.

But are they even wise elders? The Greeks have a saying: "Gray hair doesn't mean wisdom, it simply means old age." And if elders are not wise, but merely antiquated and no longer useful consumers, then what purpose do they have on a youth-based planet where pop culture and planned obsolescence rule the world? Are the elders the new pariah of cash-tism? What if technological medicine is able to push average longevity to one hundred years, while the world sees us as obsolete after sixty, or even fifty? The combination of relentless consumerism and blind technology is a troubling development of modern life.

For eons on our planet, the extended family unit was the social security system. Extended families were vital in agricultural life, with many hands making lighter work. Parents changed diapers, and they cared for their children until maturity. Children, in turn, cared for parents in old age until the time came to help them leave their bodies in a sacred and dignified manner. The cycle, again, was obvious. All the while, grandchildren would watch and learn how it was done for their turn. Then, in the relatively recent past, the nuclear family evolved to one wage earner. Today, because of economic reasons and changes in opportunity and norms, both parents work, children are sent to day care, and old parents go to rest homes, a euphemism for homes for the obsolete and out of the way.

My heart cries out that we are in dire need of more wise elders, and we need to hear from the ones we already have. There is no easy or obvious solution. But we should at least be humble and apologetic for calling our Indigenous ancestors primitive, given the exploitation and disintegration they have experienced in the face of "modernity."

If it is true that Aboriginal cultures remained "primitive" due to too much WeQ, then it is surely equally true that our modern IQ culture, in its addiction to "progress" that doesn't promote the good of all, has become environmentally and spiritually devastated. We need more wise elders to restore value to the decades remaining in a person's life after voluntary or forced retirement, sometimes at age fifty-five. We need more wise elders, activated by wisdom and justice, to work globally, across cultures and ideologies, to inspire new and sustainable ways for all of us to coexist on our planet. If the best of ancient wisdom were in sync with and talking to the best of modern science, we would undoubtedly create a more sustainable, integrated, internally enjoyable lifestyle for the largest number of people.

There remains great potential and glimpses of hope everywhere, including nestled in homes where grandparents teach the value of cooperation or speak of the sacred nature of the land or simply give a constant reminder to a child that life is not exactly as it appears to be. The world-reknowned scientist Dr. David Suzuki facilitated an Elders Forum recently in Vancouver, Canada, with the expressed purpose of finding out how elders can step up and make a difference on issues that are vital to the sustainability of the planet. And in 2004, thirteen grandmothers from Mexico, Nepal, Brazil, Tibet, Japan, Gabon, and across the United States formed the International Council of Thirteen Indigenous Grandmothers. Their goal is to uphold the teachings of our ancestors, advocate the use of traditional medicines, and protect Mother Earth.

And who are Kenyan tree planter Wangari Maathai, author/ farmer/poet Wendell Berry, and world-renowned environmental activist Vandana Shiva, if not wise elders?

Thank the Stars Above

One of the Vedic sciences associated with elders has always been a combination of astronomy and astrology—elders would spend every night for a lifetime watching the sky. Imagine the effect on the mind and soul of spending our lifetimes watching nature as much as we watch television. Start today! The ancient sciences of astronomy and Vedic astrology are light years from newspaper-style horoscope astrology, which teaches us little beyond how desperate we are for guidance and is strictly for entertainment and understandably mocked by science. The elders came from an understanding that the very nature of time is cyclic and that "what goes around comes around." Time is measured by the cycles and order of the stars and planets, including Earth. For thousands of years the sky was observed by the elders until it yielded the complex mathematical relationships of its inner workings. It became clear to them that events on Earth were timed to planetary movements, and there were subtle seasonal changes upon which agriculture also depended. Other celestial movements revealed themselves to be intertwined with specific human events on Earth.

All of this culminated in an understanding that the moment of birth reveals patterns of cause and effect traveling with each soul.

The wisest elders of all cultures have come to similar conclusions. India, in particular, has a remarkable history of Vedic astrologers and seers whose observations in the great epics can be verified by computers, revealing uncanny accuracies. Scientist Carl Sagan, in his book *Cosmos*, wrote about how the remarkable teachings of the Vedic elders so correctly corresponded with the cosmology of science: It "is the only one of the world's great faiths dedicated to the idea that the cosmos itself undergoes an immense, indeed an infinite number of deaths and rebirths.... Its cycles run from our ordinary day and night to a day and night of Brahma 8.64 billion years long, longer than the age of the earth or the sun and about half of the time since the big bang. And there are much longer time scales still."

How could they have known such things? According to the Vedas, the information was downloaded by yogis from or received during the visits of Avatars. In the film *Avatar*, the Tree of Souls holds the voices of the ancestors, their stories and their accumulated wisdom. If one "plugged in"—almost a physical representation of Yoga—the ancestral voices could actually be heard. The ancients told us this is possible. Under that sacred tree, in a mingling of cultures, Jake and Neytri unite and form their bond as husband and wife. Two cultures cross—and listen—resulting in greater wisdom and understanding. The teachings of the Avatars say that the Indigenous cultures of our ancestors are still active within us. We share the planet with them. We share genetic material with them. We share cell memory with them. We share aspirations and hopes and longings with them.

As Helen Keller once wrote, having been forced by her surroundings to have a greater inner world, "I believe in the immortality of the soul because I have within me immortal longings." Similarly, even with the subtleties of evolution, the condition of Mother Earth today is shaping us to remember and literally cultivate a different relationship with Her. As Europeans once "discovered" the New World, we are today "discovering" our ancient wisdom. The cycles continue.

Tuning In

The IQ culture's limitation is a "seeing is believing" paradigm. For the ancients, by hearing properly, it was possible to contact subtle realities that were present but could not be seen directly. This hearing power grows in twice-born elders. As their bodily senses fade and their eyes see less, their ears "see" more. The shells of our physical bodies, which at first isolate us from invisible reality and truth, gradually disintegrate. Watching our elders leave their bodies at the moment of their passing is necessary medicine for the human fear of and grief over death. The final message of the elders is that we do not die—we are relocated. There is no death, only another form of life.

But who will teach the children this truth?

The Lakota Sioux First Nations tribe of North America has a saying: "The grandparents and grandchildren are natural friends because they have the same common enemy." If we have children in day care, and lonely elders in homes, why not put the elders in charge of day care? How about a rent-a-grandparent day care center? Or why not have both young and old planting trees and flowers wherever possible? These babies and elders need to complete the link of life in each other's arms.

The stories of the Vedas say that when Avatars descend to Mother Earth, they do so to defend Her from the unbalanced and destructive actions of cruel and selfish humans. Inevitably, it is the innocent, the children, the women, and the elderly who are being harmed most by their exploiters. The Avatar—who consciously pervades all beings—feels their pain and protects them at all costs. We must try to be like the Avatars and do the same. By allowing ourselves to feel the pain of the innocent, we find our strength, our truth, our dharma. By feeling this pain, we begin to hear the Divine Mother's voice.

One of India's contemporary and well-known gurus is famous for telling his affluent students that instead of complaining about their "painful" personal lives, they should go out and serve those who are truly suffering—and once they do, to their surprise they feel much better! For the most part, we are self-centered and are not looking to serve, protect, and love all. In order to find our strength, that pure force of love, truth, and dharma, we must allow ourselves to feel the pain of the innocent.

In ancient India, the great epics tell us—or try to teach us—that when war was the last option, only the trained warriors would gather at a designated area. Farmers could be plowing their fields next door and would be safe. The warriors only fought their equals on a field of battle. One side would win. There might be a change of government, but the innocent civilians should always be protected.

Massive urbanization is taking place across the world. In the last ten years, for the first time in human history, the number of people living in cities surpassed the number in rural areas. With billions of economically disenfranchised people forced into ever-expanding slum cities without sanitation, let alone real opportunity, the horrendous number of civilians killed in war will become harder and harder to minimize.

The Avatars implore us to stand up against social injustice and feel the pain of the unprotected and, by doing so, demand their protection. The military must again protect civilians—women, children, the elderly. In ancient India, according to the epics, the great kings and queens did not eat until everybody had been fed. Those who are fortunate should always use their wisdom, strength, and resources to protect the most disadvantaged.

Our wise elders must teach the same things to our grandchildren: Protect the innocent. Protect the environment. Protect the sacred. What we need are truth-telling elders who are not on anyone's payroll, are not influenced by popularity polls, money, or some promotional corporate agenda. Our grandchildren for the next seven generations, and beyond, need this. And with the transfer of this wisdom will come the real possibility of creating a truly sustainable "social security."

NINE

FREEDOM, INDIVIDUALITY, AND LIBERATION

*Namaste, I see you leading everyone toward freedom in eternity.
You celebrate the differences that make us who we are, and you protect
the small voices trying to be heard. You know that investing in people
is the purpose of being human, while the essence of our
humanity rests on protecting all that lives.*

It has been said that if it weren't for people under the age of twenty-four, the truth would never be spoken. This is universally consistent because of the freshness and enthusiasm of youth who are not yet damaged or disappointed in life. In the Vedic culture of India, the intention was for youth to be met in this truth-telling stage by the wise elders, who from the age of seventy-five were dedicated to spiritual teaching and had no other purpose in life than to speak the highest truths to guide the next generation.

In a culture where wise elders command an audience, their truth-telling voices are the vital counterforce to the inevitably biased voices of those who are attached only to a particular profit-motivated material outcome. According to this ancient tradition, the unbiased truth telling of elders is the handmaiden of the final purpose of the Cosmic University: graduation—known in India as *Moksha*, "liberation."

The intermediate purpose of the University is to take classes—that is to say, to have life experiences—from which knowing is extracted. The etiquette or guideline for all students is Bhumi dharma: the preservation of the campus. The type of classes that are necessary to take arise from one's sva-dharma, which is the specific nature of one's body-mind complex. The deepest purpose of all this effort is to draw out the essence of one's eternal nature—the perfection of the individual atma, or one's true self. This third dharma specifically asks the biggest of questions: "What is your *true nature* once you have graduated (Moksha) from the University of material experiences—and what is next for you?" This, as was previously mentioned, is sanatan dharma, one's true nature not just in this body but eternally. Moksha states that the purpose of life on Earth is to improve the atmas and lead them toward increasing freedom until liberation is reached (also known as ultimate freedom, release from bondage, going beyond, and so on). The Avatar also teaches various paths that lead us toward freedom and liberation while we are still living on Earth.

In a culture shaped by modern material science focused upon products, and with our lives increasingly focused on perfecting our relationship with matter, this idea of liberation from matter can seem counterintuitive.

From automobiles to computers, televisions, radios, cell phones, and a host of other devices, our tools now shape and dominate our lives. We spend trillions of dollars to go out into space, with no scientific evidence there is anywhere inhabitable to go—and with the clear understanding that only a few humans could actually go anyway. It is important to remember that just because we can do something scientifically compelling, it is not necessarily a good thing to do. The question is this: "Is the purpose of life to change matter or to change ourselves?" It was Pope Pius XI who noticed that "dead matter goes into the factory and comes out improved, whereas men go into the factory and come out degraded."

What then is science's proposition as to the purpose of all living entities, including humans? Who are we really, and what is our ultimate evolutionary goal? What will help us achieve this goal? What are the obstacles? Who ultimately gives the permission to certain corporations or commodity-driven science or *anybody* to alter Mother Nature so drastically, sometimes dangerously? These questions are rarely asked.

So which is it? Are we here to improve matter, or are we here to improve ourselves? The teachings of the Avatars for thousands of years have told us that to *improve either*, we have to *understand both*. In the end, we are not ultimately here to improve matter, we are here to understand our true nature—eternal, transcendental, joyful. And learning this should always be for the good of all.

How Free Is Free?

Consider two scenarios: In one, a 747 airliner full of passengers is in midair. Someone on the plane, wearing headphones and looking at his own video screen, is watching a movie that you don't like. Should you confiscate his laptop, kill him, colonize him and take his seat, yell at him, or mind your own business and watch a movie you like?

In the second scenario, you're in the same plane again at about forty thousand feet. A passenger takes out a little barbeque, fills it with charcoal, splashes it with lighter fluid, and pulls out a pack of matches. Should you ask him what he plans to cook, tackle him to the ground as quickly as possible for putting everybody's lives at serious risk, or let him do whatever he wants because he paid for his seat?

But the more important questions are these: Are we free to attack people because we don't like what they're doing? Or must we leave them alone because they are free to do as they like, as long as what they are doing causes others no actual harm?

This is a paradox: real freedom is constrained. Real freedom needs to be defined and comes with responsibility.

So what is freedom? What does it mean to be free? What are the limitations on freedom? Why are there limitations on freedom? What within freedom is infinite? Anything?

From the Avatar's point of view, until we figure out for ourselves the nature of freedom, we are destined to be dragged along by the inherent entropy of the natural world and the whims of the beings who live here. So how do we figure out who we are, what we want, and the nature of freedom?

The answer to that question lies within our free will, but the Avatar takes the biggest view possible, with a few thought-provoking rules. The campus we live on—the UniverseCity—was created for a purpose. It is not run by a cruel, tyrannical deity. Because we are eternal, we do not have to do *everything* correctly in one lifetime. There is no eternal damnation. We are not born evil. All living beings are students with an equal right to be here. Consciously or unconsciously, we are studying this world with a view on graduating to a state of ultimate freedom, joy, and the highest possible awareness. During our stay here, we should be as free as possible to move about as long as we don't abuse that privilege and harm the campus. We should be free to think, speak, and meditate any way we like. Nature and Her renewable resources are everyone's natural gifts and are not the property of any human. This campus is in fact Mother Nature's body and does not belong to any group of students. Devas, or the Laws of Nature, are also atmas acting as staff or divine helpers in support of the campus. From this it follows that air, water, a place to live, and access to the healing resources of herbal medicines and food in the forest are the basic rights of all beings on the campus. Those here who have been empowered materially, for whatever reasons, are responsible to try and find a way for all beings to have access to uncontaminated food, air, water, healing substances, and shelter. Private use of campus resources comes with the responsibility of sustainability, stewardship, and assurance that these resources are being used for the well-being of all entities. All of these rules can be classified as Bhumi dharma.

These ideas are not to intended to endorse some naive or romanticized idea of Indigenous culture. On countless levels, we are far beyond the simplicity of natural Indigenous environments. Implementation of these ideas requires a hybrid culture—not unlike the idea of hybrid cars—as we transition to more sustainable modes of living. Nevertheless, the underlying premise of personal freedom in all of this is crucial.

And given our environmental emergency, there are a few places to begin immediately. The first starting point is the food we eat. Some of the problems are remarkably obvious. Our factory farms and food lots, all the way to the slaughterhouse, are to a significant degree torturous to animals and environmentally devastating. Our food is so processed that much of it is largely devoid of nutrition, giving rise for the first time in history to a large group of people who are simultaneously obese and malnourished. Recent statistics stated by Michael Pollan in his book *The Omnivore's Dilemma* show that forty thousand foods in a large supermarket are made from derivatives of corn, resulting not from a drive for human well-being or the health of our children but from an aggressive corn commodities market. The food-production chain itself, at every step, is also powered by and dependent upon finite and diminishing fossil fuels: the cultivating, the harvesting, the packaging, the exporting. The system is so inefficient that agribusiness (which has replaced the independent family farm) requires mass subsidization to survive. Through propaganda, and to survive, agribusiness must convince people to consume three thousand calories daily when we are, on average, a two-thousand-calorie-per-person species.

Animals Have Atmas Too!

The related but much more serious issue is meat. If a lecture on vegetarianism is expected here, it won't be happening. The Vedic culture is clear that the evolution of diet is both a geographical and personal evolutionary choice. At all times on the campus, all types and grades of learning are going on, dependent on or reacting to infinite circumstances. No one simple ideology or behavior will be right for everyone. If one's nature and geography support it, the ideal Vedic diet is vegetarian. However, it makes no sense to try to make the carnivorous Inuits be vegetarian. Similarly, the Dalai Lama, upon leaving the harsh terrain of Tibet, desperately tried to become fully vegetarian. His genetic makeup, linked to thousands of years of limited resources on the Asian steppes, would not allow it. His health suffered to the point where he is forced to occasionally eat meat. Perhaps the much more important issue is the process taken for a given animal to become meat.

The most degraded route is likely the factory farm and the multinational slaughterhouse, as mentioned earlier. As the saying goes, if slaughterhouses had glass walls, everybody would become vegetarian, or at least think about the effects of their meat-eating habits. Factory-raised animals—according to the Avatars, each also an atma here to experience life—exist in ways that would cause us to weep and protest if our own pets were subjected to conditions even remotely similar.

It's essential that we see the connection between the two, which is undeniable. Pigs, cows, and sheep, suffering their entire lives, are as intelligent and vulnerable as dogs and cats and are as hungry to live, to not suffer, and to follow their essential natures—their individual dharmas. The Avatars implore us to help protect the innocent. We must at least begin by remembering that, no matter what, it is wrong to neglect another being, so damaged by despair and injury, uncared for, unloved, desocialized, with no further experience or hope of a free and natural life.

Albert Schweitzer, the famed humanitarian doctor, asked us to "think occasionally of the suffering of which you spare yourself the sight."

It has often been said that we can have no peace on the planet until we treat our fellow beings with the dignity and compassion—even if they are killed for food—that we ourselves long for. Who could imagine that Mother Earth could be peaceful when literally billions of Her children are treated so inhumanely. Is a caged life of neglect, injury, disease, fear, and brutality truly necessary to bring food to our tables?

Neytri in the *Avatar* movie is distraught at the unnecessary deaths of the forest animals that are caused by Jake Sully's stupidity. As time goes on and Jake's Indigenous training continues, he learns to make a "clean kill"—to consciously consign the atma of a killed or hunted animal back into the All Mother, thanking the animal for its body. All Indigenous people, though in particular the forest-dwelling hunter-gatherers, understood the profound responsibility of taking a life in order to live. The daily experience of this energy cycle and the debt of respect owed to each animal eaten was palpable. Accordingly, the eating of meat would be restricted to the local supply of animals. Modern people have no such intuitive warning device on the outside of their refrigerators.

And what can be said about the dreaded *abattoirs*, a French word for slaughterhouse that sounds almost elegant. Slaughterhouses are largely unregulated. Under devastatingly cruel conditions, humans—

often poorly paid immigrants working long hours—slaughter unhappy, helpless victims by the billions. Slaughterhouses, for these obvious reasons, have a statistically high rate of employee turnover, injury, alcoholism, and drug use.

Seeing the Sacredness of All Life

In the 1970s, when I earned my degree in history and comparative religion, one of my eccentric yet clear-seeing professors taught a class on Judaism, Christianity, and Islam. One day, we took a surprise field trip up a local mountain, with my professor leading a goat and a puzzled group of students. At the top of the mountain, he took out a knife and ceremoniously sacrificed the goat to Yahweh, Jesus, and Allah, and then proceeded to skin and gut the animal, preparing it for the barbeque. Later that day the protests began. The SPCA was called and fingers were wagged. The professor took his critics to the student union cafeteria and pointed to the menu, which included beef, pork, chicken, fish, and so forth, and he asked if anyone was going to do anything about the slaughter of *those* animals.

Just as I encourage all vegetarians to at least occasionally get their hands in the dirt, to all meat eaters I recommend the periodical killing of an animal they like to eat—just to stay in touch with the process and truth of what it takes to consume animal flesh. The key to integrity is to have an understanding of how the animal lives and dies and to respond accordingly to the information. After all, all survival requires some sort of killing. That process needs to be moved toward the sacred, which results in greater compassion, sustainability, and gratitude.

The first freedom issue for animals is straightforward and comes from seeing their sentience: they should have a real and joyful life. If their lives are sacrificed for food, it must be done with integrity and the understanding of what it means to eat another being to sustain one's own life. Though some traditions do not believe animals even have souls, or atmas, it is true that they feel pain, fear, and neglect—and that they suffer. How a person, or even a nation, should face this problem has been spoken about by the greatest minds for eons. Jesus said, "Whatever you do unto the least of these, you do unto me." Thomas Edison, the great American inventor, put it this way: "Until we stop harming all other living beings, we are still savages." And finally, Mahatma Gandhi said: "The greatness of a nation and its moral progress can be judged by the way its animals are treated."

Holy Cow

The idea that Vedic practitioners in India worship the cow is inaccurate, but the cow is a symbol of divine plenty, grace, and love. The bull and the cow are revered for the endless bounty they provide in terms of calories and work. Prior to tractors, the bull was the best plow animal. From the grazing cow comes milk, cheese, cream, butter, yogurt, and ghee. The bull is also the symbol of dharma because of its strength, steadiness, and harvesting power, while the cow is the symbol of Mother Earth, who gives us energy.

Understanding the food chain and holding sustainability and animals as sacred is essential. Awareness of this allows the purchasing of food to become a political and sacred act, in which we vote with our dollars.

Namaste applies to all beings, in the hope that we begin to see all as atmas now, including the animals, struggling to find their way through this difficult University. Whenever possible, mercy, love, compassion, and, above all, the progression of every atma should motivate all we do. At any given moment, we are surrounded by atmas, often in bodies we don't recognize, others we can't see at all. For all we know, some are the parents, lovers, or children we swore to always love in a previous life. Taking the bigger view, all we do should be directed toward the good of all beings, seeing beyond their skin color, thoughts, present deeds, illusions, or confusion, and we should help them to move forward whenever possible. It is said in both the Vedas and in the film *Avatar*, "our great mother Eywa does not take sides, Jake, only protects the balance of life." We cannot graduate from the University until we learn to understand and treat every living being as divine in essence. Holding the well-being of all atmas in one's heart makes a person a *Mahatma* [ma-ha-at-ma], meaning "great soul." One of the great hopes in Pandora's Box is that because we are eternal, we can repeat life again and again and again until we are ready for Moksha for graduation day. This makes life not only relentlessly hopeful but also the ultimate Olympic event, and just getting to the Olympics is a miracle.

We must push forth through cynicism, cruelty, and uncertainty to be as strong and upright as the tree, to offer a true namaste to all beings. As the world's resources and patience are stretched, we must seek to be more caring, discerning, altruistic, and generous. For in the words of Mahatma Gandhi, "The Lord has provided enough for everyone's need, but not enough for everyone's greed."

TEN

YOGA—THE LINK, THE BOND, THE UNION

Namaste, I see you as divinely connected to everything, united with and linked to all, your balance and integrity teach by example the eternal truths you embody. You are now the same in essence as the effulgent divines whose sacred forms you adore in mystic meditation.

There is a famous story from India in which six blind men are asked to examine an elephant and report their findings. One of them touches the side of the elephant and says it is a wall. Another touches a leg and reports the elephant is a pillar. The next blind man holds the tail and pronounces it is a broom. Yet another holds the elephant's trunk and reports it is a snake. The fifth blind man grasps the elephant's tusk and declares it to be a mighty weapon. The sixth blind man, feeling hairs all over the skin, concludes it is a rug. Here comes the eternal question: which blind man is right? The answer is *all and none*. Each seer is partially right, which is often further simplified to "It's all one," or "We are all one," or "All paths lead to the same place," which again are only partial truths.

Managing fallout from disagreement over "the truth" is very important. If the six began to quarrel over their findings, it would be useful to remind them that the subject is very big, so each only sees part of the answer, and therefore they should peacefully share our conclusions without harming one another over our differences. "The truth *is* one, but visions of it are many" is another way to express this. This is the well-known "Unity amidst Diversity" slogan, for which India is so justly famous. But who is really right? They *all* are. Then who is wrong? They all are.

Ah, then it's all the same? No—but it is all connected.

Oh, so it *is* all one? Yes, in one sense, yet every part is simultaneously different. This is the cosmic version of "I see you—Namaste." Welcome to the PhD program—where we grow by engaging with paradox and finally deal with the big questions of human existence.

Believing Is Seeing

The Library of Vedic Visions has been accumulated this way and refined over many thousands of years as a systematic curriculum with a view toward empowering students with the ability to "see." In the Vedas, there are six subjects for atmas—six angles of vision on "the truth"—and they are called *darshans*, or ways of seeing. The six schools of Vedic philosophy, known as the six darshans, are as follows:

1. *Sankhya*: **General Science**—The study of matter itself in all of its categories, including its male and female characteristics

2. *Nyaya*: **Logic**—The study of logic and correct thinking

3. *Vaishesika*: **Atomic Physics**—Examining the atoms and the molecular structure of all matter

4. *Yoga*: **Techniques of Meditation**—Making the link that allows us to connect with all things and to understand their

true essences, culminating in reestablishing our link to the Transcendental

5. *Purva Mimansa*: **Rituals**—The use of rituals and mantras as direct links to the Devas, to perfect action in this world, and to make a direct connection to the unseen realities

6. *Uttara Mimamansa*: **Vedanta**—The end or goal toward which the Vedic knowledge is leading, Vedanta concludes by describing the ultimate Transcendental reality

Each of the six darshans could make up its own book, but I'll quickly summarize them here. The first is the study of matter in all its forms. The second is logic and certain rules and skills of thinking. The third way is an atomic and molecular way of seeing things. Thinkers in India have long included small-particle thinking in the understanding of this world of matter. Yoga is the fourth stage, which teaches us to understand the essence of everything—not just as theory but also through direct connection. It is especially aimed at empowering individuals with the ability to form a link or connection of direct experience between themselves and anything with which they are in contact. Yoga is the stage in seeing where each student, starting with the physical and moving toward the invisible realms both here and beyond, is taught how to have a direct experience of the *true essence* of everything with which they come in contact. Not only is Yoga the art of linking with ourselves and the object of our focus, it is also the bridge that connects the first three darshans, which mainly describe our relationship with matter. The fifth and sixth visions inform us about the higher beings and the Transcendental reality that is not directly visible here.

In *Avatar*, the notion of linking and connecting was presented in many provocative and visual ways. The first of these is the very basis of Yoga practice. The idea of linking, connecting, plugging in, and forming a link stem from some of the diverse meanings of the Sanskrit word *yoga*, which comes from the root word *yuj*, which is pronounced like the English word *huge*. In the film, the Indigenous people of Pandora live with a conscious and focused connection to everything around them. When surrounded by so many complex living things, listening to them and coming to a cooperative understanding is a daily opportunity, challenge, and survival skill. We postindustrial people often live in inorganic urban environments with less obvious need for attention to live connections. In a big city, most people have a small circle of human friends, a few co-workers, and maybe a pet—and studiously ignore the other millions of humans all around them. People often don't even know their nearest neighbor. If most city dwellers were taken from their concrete jungle and dropped down in a Pandora-like forest, they would be just as "stupid" as the inept Jake Sully is. Suddenly he is surrounded by a multitude of things that must be connected with rather than ignored. Was it Jake's "ignor-ance" of how to connect and link that made him—and makes us—seem so ignorant of the ways of the heart and of nature? Just to survive, Aboriginals from a young age received WeQ training which taught them how to be a yogi—how to connect and link to everything around them and within them.

Stretching the Mind

People tend to think that yoga is only body postures, flexibility, and possibly breathing. This is understandable since that is how it's generally presented at Western yoga studios. But Yoga has a vast universal meaning. In *Avatar*, when Jake is first transferred from his paralyzed human body to his powerful, vital, Pandorean body, he runs in joy and then digs his toes into the soil, fully connecting with his new body and the ground beneath him. This is highly and intentionally metaphoric. Before that moment, Jake was part of the epidemic among modern humans, which finds us increasingly detached from our bodies. Humans spend their days and often their nights staring at a computer or television screen.

The philosopher Descartes said, "I think; therefore I am." Did he lead us unknowingly to our present disembodied condition, where living vicariously through characters on a screen seems normal? Is that why the Pandoreans called the human invaders "Dream Walkers"? The point is, Yoga does not begin with *thinking*; it begins with training individuals how to be *fully present* in their own bodies.

Since we are eternal atmas going from body to body, from lifetime to lifetime, we can compare that experience to trading in an old car and buying a new one. I call this "re-in-*car*-nation." And if you did buy a new car, a really great one, let's say a Ferrari, what would be the first thing you would do?

I hope the answer is: read the owner's manual. It would be a shame if you ruined your beautiful car due to unnecessary ignorance of its needs and specifications. That's why it is so profoundly important to know your own essential nature (or sva) and your "operating system" (or dharma). Sva-dharma is one of the three teachings the Avatar says we need to know to be successful in life. But in our modern culture, we teach often very rough and potentially harmful sports. We sometimes push children to compete too hard, to drive their bodily vehicles too fast, while failing to train them in long-term "system maintenance." Who out there helps them find their "user's manual" and understand their "body type"? (Ayurvedic medicine is the science that specifically identifies all body types and their specific user's manuals.)

In Yoga and its companion science, Ayurvedic medicine, the *first* learning of your embodiment is the means to identify your specific body type (because every body is different). Put another way, it's learning how to sit comfortably in your car.

Yoga is a science with eight departments teaching us how to link with everything. The final goal of Yoga is to link with that which is beyond our seeing, but the linking begins where we are—living in a particular make and model of vehicle.

Going Out on a Limb

These eight aspects of Yoga are called "limbs." The first limb is called asana. To drive a car you must first sit in the driver's seat in just the right posture or position. So the various poses or postures of yoga are intended to balance your vehicle (body type), to make sure all the systems are flowing and integrated. Once that balance is achieved and all systems are go, you can sit in your driver's seat comfortably for a long ride. That final steady "seat" is the ultimate body posture, or asana. In that perfect seat, one can sit comfortably for a long time and meditate.

Anyone who has regularly ridden horses has to appreciate Jake's horseback training in *Avatar*, which the Na'vi call "forming the bond." I have ridden and trained horses much of my life, so I can say with some authority that if you get on the back of a powerful horse without linking and forming "the bond," you will soon be on your own back looking up at the horse. Amateur riders often "talk" to their horses in human speech: "Nice horsey, easy now." But horses talk energy. They feel what the rider wants; they hear the rider's emotions and sense anxiety or desires. Knowledgeable riders "talk" with the horse through their prana, or life force. Or as it was put in *Star Wars*, "Use the Force, Luke." The part *Star Wars* forgot to teach is that prana is controlled by the breath—by how we breathe. The Sanskrit word for "control" is *yama*, and the second limb of Yoga is called pranayama: "breath control of the life force."

The secret with horses is to breathe with them, to "tell them" with long, deep, slow breaths that everything is fine. Horses hear or feel this as, "Easy now, be calm, everything is fine." And when hearing that thought, they relax and realize that both they and you are safe. They then release control to you and, by relaxing, blend their energy with yours. This is the bond. Once learned, the forming of this bond can be consciously pursued with any other "air-breathing being" or jiva atma. This is what Jake Sully learns—and we all can—giving him a little more Indigenous "horse sense" learned straight from the horse's mouth.

Let's tie this together with a metaphor from the Vedas to help us see it better. This example comes from the *Upanishads*—the philosophical "forest teachings" of the Avatars. The Vedas reveal that the body is like a chariot (car); our senses (smell, taste, touch, sight, and hearing) are like horses (the horsepower is our engine); the mind is the reins (steering wheel connecting us to our horse senses); the driver is our discernment (the chauffeur and navigation system); and we, the atmas, are the passengers (reincarnated again).

When we were children, our elders would say, "Hold your horses." What the yogi learns is that the body (the horse/five senses) is nervous and uncertain and is waiting for the signal from the driver and passenger—you—that everything is okay. Modern science calls this the "fight or flight syndrome." Prana, or breath, is the secret to calming both the body and the mind.

The next two limbs of Yoga are crucial. They are called *yams* and *niyams*. They include trying to cause as little harm as possible, truth telling, cleanliness, contentedness, restraining from gluttony, and so on. Think of them as the dos and don'ts of both your vehicle (your body) and the traffic laws of the road. Being a person wanting to work with the ritam, the Laws of Nature, you wouldn't want the "Skyway Patrol" (Devas or Laws of Nature) to pull you off the road for breaking the natural laws. We also need to use the right fuel (meat, alcohol, drugs, and many other chemical substances that disturb the system are generally not recommended). Also, it is vital to learn to service your vehicle correctly (body care) or it will likely break down before your "human race" is finished. Yams and niyams are the rules of the road and the specifications of your body.

Freedom 101

I see you, your eternal atma, sitting in your body and wondering, *Why don't we just rise up into the sky and fly wherever we want?* If the flying scenes in *Avatar* were your first official, waking, "out of the body" experience, send an email to James Cameron and thank him for putting modern special effects to such tantalizing use. Perhaps while in dreams you have had out-of-body trips, or on a spring day, watching the wild flight of a hawk or eagle. But either way, tell me, who wouldn't want to ride on one of Pandora's birds? All experienced yogis know these "out of body flights," and, as far as I know, no one has captured the feeling of flying on film as well as James Cameron.

But let me see if I can make this process simple, and explain what it means. At the moment of death, we must leave our bodies, whether we want to or not. So when they tow your car off to the junk yard, it's always good to have a Plan B. This is death. Seeing as we're at a University, the yogis put it this way: "Life is a class and death is the final exam."

The purpose of Yoga is to live in a way that leaves you clear and self-directing *at the moment* your body is up for recycling. That takes practice. Let's just say that your atma can fly but has forgotten that it can. Our wings atrophy from riding in a car for too long. Even if the journey is enjoyable, the question remains: where will you go next?

The first four limbs of Yoga are meant to teach us how to live in the most cooperative way while we are here on Earth and linked to

Mother Nature. The next four limbs are going to teach us how to fly, and not just in our minds, but to really set our own destinations for our next births—either in the University of Matter or even to graduate and fly away from the material world altogether. What if, after this current birth and life, advanced human life included within it your choice of where to go next? Which would you prefer: to choose your own vacation (spiritual destination), to not be able to choose at all, or to end up somewhere you may not even like? It's your consciousness, and Yoga says we can learn to fly and chose our own paths, our own divine destinations, but having a guide increases the chances of having a great vacation. If you are willing to expand your thinking, this is the "Guru's Flight School." It doesn't even matter if you crash a few times; in fact, it's almost a given that you will. But we are eternal and we cannot die. This is where we see you. Namaste—and welcome aboard. It's time to learn to fly—transcendentally.

The outer and inner realms of our experiences are not opposed to each other. They are complementary—two real sides of the same coin. Thousands of years ago, India mastered inner space flight just as certainly as we have now gone to outer space. For shamans and yogis, inner flying is as real and available as flying in an airplane. I'm not referring here to levitating yogis. I'm talking about flying to other realms or dimensions. The Vedas say there are fourteen material-world dimensions. In modern physics, string theory suggests there are eleven. Even if yogis and physicists do not necessarily find common ground here, both agree that there are many dimensions to the Universe.

The function of Yoga as a darshan or a way of seeing is to begin to turn our gaze inward. To do this, we need to learn to unplug our senses from the addicting and compelling (and beautiful) outer world and turn our attention entirely to the inner realm of experience. We need to put on the blinders, park our horses—and forget about them completely—in order to go within. Don't worry, they will still be there when we return.

This fifth limb of Yoga is called *pratyahara*: "withdrawing our senses from their outer objects and turning them inward." This is also called the "power of the turtle." Just as the turtle has the ability to withdraw its head, tail, and limbs into its shell, so a yogi learns to withdraw awareness from the outer world of sensation and experience, and redirect awareness toward the inner dimensions of reality. Unconsciously, we do a similar thing each night when sleep overtakes us for the mandatory maintenance of the "vehicle." While the body is parked, we are temporarily free to roam about the highways and byways of inner space—and we do.

Inside Out

Most people think that the physical, external world of experience is real and the inner world is unreal. Yogis say both are real and that both are connected to higher levels of reality. Yoga is the pursuit of those higher realms and the freedom that comes from their discovery. This may not at all fit most preconceived ideas of Yoga, but that's a great thing—because there's nothing better than a little mind expansion on the road to spiritual growth.

The sixth limb of Yoga is understandable to people simply as something we all do every day. This limb is called *dharana*, or "one pointedness of the mind." In the outer world, it's self-evident that success in most endeavors demands single-minded focus. Aiming, targeting, and holding a focus are all practice for achieving dharana within. We also understand how difficult staying focused in the outer world is amid endless distractions. Going *within* and holding one thought or one point of focus is the most difficult form of one-pointedness. Sleep, in a way, can offer this focus in the form of dreams. But to go within, and to focus deeply, *without* sleeping is to do a similar shift in consciousness and yet be more awake than at any other time.

Yogis tell us that when leaving our body at the time of death, the chaos of physical disintegration makes holding a focus extremely difficult and unlikely. Once the body is shed, we are alone inside the mind—a "hall of mirrors" where single-pointed, purposeful focus is stunningly difficult to achieve, let alone maintain for long periods of time. Without long-term focus training, one's subtle airplane rarely leaves the hangar, let alone takes flight.

This singular focus of dharana is supposed to be a relaxed state, yet one still maintaining complete focus. Yoga describes this undivided attention as holding complete focus with no tension. It is compared to a dam holding water, with no strain or effort. All of the first limbs and effortless internal attention to a single focus are prerequisite skills to truly practicing the seventh limb of Yoga. The first six limbs must first be achieved.

The Sanskrit for the seventh limb of Yoga is *dhyan*. Alongside Buddhist thought, which arose in northern India and then migrated East, this word became *chan* in China and then *zen* in Japan. The word is often translated in English as "meditation"—which has become a loose and casual definition of the word. Meditation is often used to mean empty of ordinary thought or inner awareness or focusing on the light and so on. In the traditional yogic meaning of the word, none of this is considered to be dhyan.

These limbs of Yoga are defined in the most concise and practical manual for yogic principles, *The Yoga Sutras* of Patanjali—Patanjali being the author. In these Yoga *sutras*, the three aims or processes of Yoga are described. The first is *tapasya*, meaning "you must do something over time with great intensity." *Tapas* means "heat (results) generated by extremely focused behaviors." It is as if our bones are made of iron. Yoga says tapasya can heat the practitioner to the point that he or she can be reshaped and go beyond previous limitations.

The second process or activity of Yoga is *svadhyaya*. As in sva-dharma, *sva* means "one's own." In this case, Yoga is *not* asking, "What is the make and model of your car?" The question is deeper: "Who are you in eternity when you are no longer covered in a material mind or body?" In other words, who are we under all the goo, under the dark covering of matter? Who is the real you? The process of learning to see one's real self, under all circumstances, is called svadhyaya.

The third action of Yoga is called *Isvara pranidhan. Isha* means "those Divine beings greater than oneself." *Pranidhan* means "to recognize, honor, and show respect to, in the proper amount." This brings us to one of the most misunderstood topics in India and almost all Indigenous cultures: the Devas, or Ishas. These are what are called by nonpractitioners and other religious groups "many gods." These "many gods" are supposedly "worshipped" by the pagans instead of offering worship and devotion to the "Real God." The three major Middle Eastern/Abrahamic religions—Judaism, Christianity, and Islam, but in particular the latter two—have been certain that the Hindus of India are worshipping many gods. As an elder of the Vedic dharma, I must say that this is inaccurate. While describing the third aim of Yoga, I'll explain why and help set the record straight. It will be up to you to decide about the difference of opinions and views.

To begin with—and this is critical—the Devas are neither gods nor competing gods. Even some Hindu/Vedic scholars have translated Deva as "demigod." This, too, is incorrect. The Devas are divine *helpers* who work on behalf of the Supreme Being (and on behalf of all the beings here). They are, metaphorically, the teachers and staff at the University of Matter. The teachers at the University should not be confused with or considered in competition with the president of the University.

Undeniably, India has thousands of names for the Supreme Being, but those initiated in the dharma understand that the Devas are all serving both us and, ultimately, the Supreme Being. Further, Devas are *atmas like us*. The Devas are divine workers who deserve our respect and appreciation (and cooperation) but not in the way worship is used with regard to the Ultimate and Supreme Source of All.

As mentioned earlier, the Devas are the Laws of Nature. Using only one's IQ vision, they appear as mathematics, as the ritam. But using our 3rd IQ vision, if we were to meet them face-to-face, they would appear in ways that our human minds might have difficulty grasping. The process of "learning to know and correctly respect the Devas," those Ishas or Rulers of Nature, is called Ishvara pranidhan.

The difference between IQ vision, WeQ vision, and 3rd IQ vision is similarly evident when we relate human-to-human. Upon first meeting, external qualities show you something about who others are. Once you get to know their inner person, the intimacy deepens, and who they really are becomes more evident. Put another way: "You can't judge a book by its cover." According to the Vedas, the external Laws of Nature are a cover for an entire realm of consciousness—they are loving beings who work for and do not compete with the Supreme Being.

To understand the underlying differences between these extremely great beings, yogis go through a curriculum of detailed mantras. For the yogi, each mantra comes with a mental image of a Deva (all the way up to the Supreme Being) as well as an explanation of the Deva's powers, laws, and actions. This is an internal vibratory science that facilitates the gradual ascent of our relating to greater and greater beings who help guide our spiritual evolution as mentors and teachers. The computer screen covered with icons is a good metaphor for mantras and images of Devas. A mantra, by its vibrational power and specific wording, leads us toward a very specific being, not unlike the way clicking an icon on a computer screen leads us to a very specific program. To think that the icons (Devas) are competing with one another, and then to get rid of them all in favor of just one giant program, would be self-defeating. This is how the yogis see the outer world and look within and beyond that world. They see great Divine beings surrounding them everywhere. The yogis put it this way: "A yogi is someone who realizes he or she is never alone."

Born Free

This brings us to the last limb of Yoga, which is called *samadhi*. The Sanskrit *sam* gave us the English word "same." Samadhi means "to become the same as that upon which you meditate." Put another way, the final stage of yogic meditation is when the essence and power of what you meditate upon is absorbed by the meditator and incorporated into your very being. According to the yogis, at this stage of the eight limbs of Yoga, the practitioner could prepare to take birth in the next life as a Deva or continue on to the subtlest boundary of the realms of the material world. At the end of this stage, Devas are groomed for the next step, beyond Yoga. That step is actually the leap our atma takes to the Transcendental Brahman, beyond our imagination or the realms of matter.

Due to the wonder of our free will, the potential for achieving higher states of manifestation exists within human beings. The study of Yoga is part of becoming more empowered and perfecting this journey. With that freedom, we can choose to associate with anyone or anything available to us. Yogis understand this remarkable rule as "whatever you associate with, you become like."

The honing of skills and perfections, of course, is a double-edged sword. As is evident all over the world, knowledge and skill can be used for benefit or for harm. That's why the teachings of the Avatar are so important: the sword of our powers is meant to be contained in the sheath of our caring for the good of all. Think of the Devas in the same way. They are simultaneously masters of a subject—certain Laws of Nature—and divine helpers working for the good of all.

When we yogis meditate upon the Devas and vibrate their mantras—their computer desktop icons, and we are starting them up—we associate with them and actually come to know them. Eventually, we even become the "same" as them (the real meaning of samadhi), and their perfections and concerns for the good of all are transferred to us, making us more perfected. In Sanskrit, that skill or empowerment is called *siddhi*. This is good because it improves us and we learn to cooperate with the Laws of Nature. Nevertheless, as eternal atmas, we are supposed to eventually graduate from this program. In the fourth pada (chapter) of *The Yoga Sutras*, Patanjali warns us: "If a Deva should come and tell you in your meditation that your Yoga is great, don't listen." Yogis are warned not to seek powers from their association with the Devas. The teacher wants the student to go beyond these powers because those material powers often lead to further material attachment. Association with the Devas is a step in our evolution, and we are improved in their company, but as the Avatars tell us, beyond that, there is much, much more.

As eternal souls, we have the potential within us to form the bond and fly. Forming this bond is what the eight limbs of Yoga and the three actions of Yoga teach us. This Yoga is one of the great secret teachings of the Avatars. It is intended to raise your autonomy and independence as you move higher in the University PhD program. In this case, the PhD stands for Pursuing our Highest Delight. This learning can reawaken our true and full potential, so we finally reach moksha—freedom, liberation of the atma—the ability to fly to anywhere we want.

ELEVEN

The Great Leap to the Transcendental Realms

Namaste, I see you poised on the peak of possibility,
eyes upon the Transcendental goal, leaping bravely, your fears gone.
Your eyes and mind are clear, and they are unwavering in their determination
to return to the timeless realms where beauty and love never fade.

In this chapter, we really are taking a grand leap. We'll be moving through the three most advanced Transcendental paths yogis can choose, both during life and at that the moment of death, so if grasping it feels difficult, it should. It's Vedanta, the sixth and final darshan (vision)—the PhD program of transcendental flight. So be kind to yourself. I'd recommend reading this chapter again when you have a chance, and then again when you have another chance. Being Vedic, the knowledge will find a way of activating inside you. And with that, I offer you this humble taste of eternal wisdom.

The Vedas contain stories and accounts of the realms beyond matter that can reawaken the memory of who we are and where we are from. For the atma, this reawakening establishes a new direction for the final goal of human life, illustrated in the sixth darshan called Vedanta—"the final vision," which can offer a new way for you, the atma, to look at and live in the world.

There is also a psychological premise for approaching this process of discerning between the atma and the body, and for graduating from our longtime association with matter. As human beings, our time in matter has always manifested as some kind of story. This story can be summed up as an unfolding plot in which each one of us is the main character in a movie largely of our own making. In short, we are each a work in progress. But even though everything within matter is temporary, beginning students get totally trapped in their own stories. The closer we get to graduating, the less we believe our "material stories," or that our minds and bodies are the real us.

Think of your story and all your memories of past events in this and previous lives as a collection of mementos—the boxes in your basement, full of old yearbooks, love letters, and photographs. To leave this world, we have to not only let go of all the joys and sorrows of the past, but we must give up our attachments *to any future outcome within matter*. A common fear of detaching from the outcome of the material story is that it will lead to inaction, to doing nothing. However, the last stage of learning within matter is the ability to do *everything* without attachment to matter, with your third eye (as in 3rd IQ) firmly focused on the Transcendental goal. This, my friends, takes practice.

Here Comes the Sun

Before discussing how to enter the Transcendental, one more metaphor will help in understanding the transition from one form of yourself to another. The Vedas reveal that our atmas are illuminating the matter of our minds and physical bodies the same way the Sun lights up the Earth. In other words, ever since your atma entered into the material world, "your spiritual form" has been lying dormant while shimmering its consciousness into your body as the body's animating principle. Material life is driven by the atma's awareness, but we have forgotten the atma.

Ramayana

Both silently vowed that this was their only love. Soon thereafter,
they were standing together in front of the sacred fire reciting
the holy vows of a lifetime commitment to each other.

It was a paradise in the center of the mighty forest. There Lakshman built a cottage, which was their home in exile; a lovelier forest retreat could not be imagined. There the faithful vulture Jataya guarded Sita while Ram and Lakshman hunted.

Ravana hatched a plan: his henchman Maricha would take the form of a jewel-encrusted magical deer and appear before Sita at their cottage as a distraction. The plan worked, and Ram chased after the alluring deer.

Sita's compassion for the thirsty sage overwhelming her good judgment, she offered water to the disguised asura, and in so doing, her hand reached oustide the circle.

In a moment, she was thrown roughly into Ravana's chariot, which rose up and began to fly away.

Once the monkey army assembled, Ram wrote his name on huge boulders, which would then float on the water's surface. With these floating rocks, the army built the bridge to Lanka.

The final confrontation between Lord Ram and the mighty Ravana ended with Ram shooting an arrow while chanting a famous mantra to the Sun.

The arrow stuck Ravana in the heart, and he fell to the ground.

At the coronation of Ram and Sita, with Lakshman standing near, Hanuman—the embodiment of pure truth, dharma, and devotion—came forward, and Mother Sita, the Mother of All, placed a necklace of pearls over Hanuman's head as a symbol of his courage and devotion.

Mahabharata

Looking in Krishna's mouth, his mother saw the entire universe—endless planets, galaxies, the vastness of space, all beings, the creator, everything!

Deep in the forest, Krishna began to play enchanting and magical melodies on his flute. Hearing this music, Radha and the gopis realized that the dance was about to begin.

As Krishna left Vrindavan, Radha and the gopis stood in the path of the chariot with tears in their eyes. In their company, Shri Krishna had revealed the deepest secrets of the atma's eternal love with the Supreme Being.

Krishna personally killed his evil uncle Kamsa. The prophecy was fulfilled.
Krishna then released Kamsa's father from prison
and restored him as the righteous King of Mathura.

At that moment a miracle happened. Krishna, the Supreme Being, incarnated as unlimited yards of sari material, and Dushasana was unable to humiliate Draupadi in front of the assembly.

Before going to his tent to take a nap, Krishna told Arjuna and Duryodana that the first one he saw upon waking would get the first choice of him or his army. In this way, Shri Krishna became the chariot driver for Arjuna.

Krishna pulled the chariot of Arjuna to the middle of the field and began to speak the words that have inspired billions of souls around the world.

Neither Krishna nor Radha, his eternal counterpart,
would ever forget the mystery and magic of their full-moon dances together,
which would always be visible in the starlit sky of their hearts.

Yoga is the gradual process of reawakening our direct perception of our spiritual bodies and burning away (releasing) any residual desires for attachment to the gu. This goo—the body/matter—is a sticky, static, unconscious substance that has been our "avatar" (in the computer-gaming sense) for having experience within matter—which, as we have seen, is different than the bigger meaning of Avatar. As for Yoga, the last step of the process is to enter the decompression chamber and remove our diving equipment in preparation for resurfacing in the Transcendental realm, similar to how Jake Sully emerges from his chamber to become the Avatar in the film.

Ode to Joy

The Vedas describe our atmas as eternal, fully conscious, and joyful by nature. So to the extent that we forget our true nature, we become affected or, more precisely, infected by certain inevitable qualities of matter—unconsciousness, suffering, and death. The universal experience of transcendentalists is that the less they are *endarkened* by matter, the more joyful they feel—not occasionally but constantly. The less attached they become to matter—their stories—the more enlightened they become and the more they recover their natural state of being permanently joyful.

The Vedic learning is not a faith-based religious tradition. It is a curriculum with processes; it is a body of evidence and teachings received by great spiritual scientists, downloaded from the great Avatars. Once they receive these teachings or initiations from a learned guru (professor) trained in these practices, the students need to practice the knowledge in order to obtain the scientific result.

A book like this or a qualified teacher can supply the tools by which many others in the past have reached the Transcendental. But only with the practice of those yogic techniques can one begin to experience the teachings. Considering that the Ultimate Avatars descend to this world from the Transcendental, it should be no surprise that adhering with great enthusiasm to their methods might be necessary to produce the intended, expansive results. We can examine only a few waves from the ocean of this eternal truth. Indeed, even the great Vedas admit to being only one river flowing down from its ocean of Transcendental greatness.

The Many Doors

The first experience of Transcendental existence is called, in Sanskrit, *Nirvana*. *Van* means "one who possesses or owns," and *nir* means "nothing." In material consciousness, we generally believe that one who owns the most objects of pleasure has the most happiness.

Ironically, in our material stage of learning, we are practitioners of goo yoga. We are wrongly convinced that someday, somehow, if we can just gather enough of the right material products, and link or join ourselves to matter, we will finally reach the state of ultimate pleasure. We will be satisfied. May I ask how that's going? Everywhere we look, people are seeking ultimate pleasures this way. People are diligently practicing all kinds of extra limbs of yoga, linking up with temporary passions: ice cream yoga, money yoga, sex yoga, drug yoga, and so on.

This is no surprise even to the transcendentalist. Every atma wants pleasure, bliss, and satisfaction, so naturally we try to fulfill these desires by first pleasing our senses, then our minds, and then finally through everything at once. Granted, it may be more enjoyable to be miserable and rich than miserable and poor, but historical testimony has shown us over and over again, from kings and queens to tyrants, tycoons, heirs, and movie and rock stars, that no amount of material experience creates permanent pleasure.

It is for this reason that the first Transcendental path—Nirvana—unfolds from a reverse or deconstructive logic. Almost everyone in the world is working hard all the time to get more material pleasure, but very few are happy, and none will become permanently satisfied. Seeing this, some conclude that matter is temporary and the only solution is to give it up entirely. Perhaps the most famous renouncer was Gautama Buddha, a wealthy Vedic prince from northern India.

Buddha: The Great Discerner

As a boy, Buddha was kept in the palace, intentionally pampered, far from the realities of the outside world. One day he secretly left the palace with a servant, and what he saw shocked him. He heard a woman giving birth, screaming in pain; he saw a disfigured man with a terrible disease; he saw another person bent and crippled with old age; finally, he saw a dead body being cremated. From his observations, Buddha concluded that the world is a place of suffering caused by everyone's *desire for and attachment to matter*, which is temporary and therefore unsatisfactory. Thus, Nirvana as taught by the Buddha is the liberation that comes from not owning any matter or having any material desires.

The most extreme followers of this path would wear the most rudimentary, unsown clothes and basic sandals, and their only possession would be a wooden begging bowl. Once a day they would go from home to home begging for leftovers. The Nirvana-seeking monks would fulfill their only material need for the day by accepting whatever food was offered (preferably vegetarian). Clearly, a person desiring and addicted to material pleasure would find this life miserable. But for those ready for this path, it relieved them of all unnecessary material worries and stresses. Strange to most of us, these monks evidently experienced constant joy and freedom far more intensely than they had from any previous material engagements.

The process of reaching Nirvana as a final goal was more deconstructive, more of a negation, than other paths intended. The monks would proceed by asking not who they were, but who they were not. The Sanskrit for this is *neti neti* or "not this, not that"—the process of examining every piece of material goo, one glop at a time, and discarding all that is temporary (and all of it is temporary). The path of striving for Nirvana in the Transcendental realm is a "reverse engineering" program where every last spec of matter must go. As the process continues, its effect—the sense of enlightenment and freedom—increases. When finally no longer *endarkened* or disturbed by matter in any way, those who achieve Nirvana exclaim, "*Gate gate pāragate pārasamgate bodhi svāhā*," which is Sanskrit for "gone, gone, gone beyond, gone beyond beyond and given to pure knowing."

In material consciousness, we are aspiring to the highest material pleasure. The yogi knows this ultimate pleasure is unattainable *in matter*. The inimitable and great Buddha, with unending compassion, devoted his life to bringing both relief from suffering and joy of liberation to every atma.

From a Vedic point of view, the Buddhist approach is a sort of healing cosmic addiction clinic, where humans finally purge all of their attachments and desires for the material world. However, because the process concludes with who we are *not*, more than with who we *are*—and even though the concept of Nirvana does occur in the Vedas—it is seen as a profound yet intermediate step of liberation, rather than the final destination. Several crucial Vedantic questions remain unanswered: Where has all this reality come from? What is its source? Why did individuality arise? What is its highest *positive* form or expression? Who are we *in eternity*? And where do we exist for eternity? Fortunately, detailed answers to these questions have been downloaded to us by the great Avatars and received by the greatest of mystics and Vedic sages.

Make Me One with Everything

The second experience of the Transcendental realm is called *Akshara Brahman*. *Akshara* means "imperishable, indestructible, enduring, and immortal." *Brahman* is from the Sanskrit root *Briha*, meaning "that fully conscious existence that is eternally expanding and full without limits" and "the luminous source of all we experience" as well as "externally full of all that is *beyond* our current experience." In this way, the Vedas indicate, a Brahman cannot be known either through investigating matter or rejecting matter, as in the Nirvanic process. And unlike the notion of Nirvana—an empty state after shedding all material concepts—Brahman is the full shining light of eternal existence. For this reason, Brahman is also called *Brahmajyoti*, or the "light of eternal, conscious and joyful existence."

Inconceivably, although Brahman is full and eternally expanding, it is simultaneously said to be ever free of all dualities, oppositions, and contradictions. So even though the many parts of matter suggest a fragmentation or duality in existence, and despite such appearances, the Vedas say that Brahman remains as a singular and undivided existence. In short, meditation on the meaning of Brahman is vital for the aspiring transcendentalist. As for the atmas—our true, eternal nature—we are both eternally part of and from that Brahman existence. Just as we experience space surrounding ourselves and the planets and the stars in our Universe, so the limitless and effulgent sky of Brahman extends *everywhere* without limitation, constituting and encompassing everything.

Our many material universes are described in the Vedas as trillions upon trillions of temporary abodes, arising and merging back into the unbounded and joyful Brahman reality—the endless sky of positive existence. In addition, it is the eternal sound vibration om that is described in the Vedas as the sound manifestation of this Brahman reality.

According to the Vedas, and as we saw with Nirvana, to remember and reenter the Brahmanic state, the atma must throw off or disidentify with matter. In Sanskrit this positive ultimate destination is described as *Aham Brahmasmi* or "I am identical with, the same in nature as, the Brahman existence." Knowing this and chanting the mantra aum, the atma can graduate from the material University, reenter the effulgent Brahman atmosphere, and then merge into Its Nature which, it turns out, is identical with our own.

This Vedantic view of our atmas' being identical with Akshara Brahman was popularized for the last twelve hundred years or so by the many students of the great teacher of Vedanta, Adi Shankara. The great professors of Vedic wisdom would assemble a thesis and commentary drawn from key statements made in all Vedic texts. These views were not academic presentations of abstract truth; they were maps to the final goal, including instructions on how to make the final step from matter back to the Transcendental realm. Throughout the world, religions, philosophers, and mystics have all practiced and experienced this om vibration and envisioned themselves as reentering the great Light of Eternity. This truth of our oneness with the Source of All has spread out from India like a golden beacon for millennia.

The slogan that summarizes Shankara's monistic revelation of our true nature is *Jagat Mithya, Brahma Satya*. The translation: "The world of matter is a mirage whereas the realm of Akshara Brahman exists eternally." The Avatars tell us this is so: that all the atmas are identical with the Akshara Brahman. Yet even at this stage of awareness, questions remain unanswered by both the emptiness of Nirvana and by the merging of ourselves into the Golden Light of Brahman.

Question One: If individuality is not part of our final, eternal conclusion, why and from where did individuality arise in the first place?

Question Two: From where did the forms of endless beauty and personal loving existence arise? In short, why are we individuals, and where did our attraction to and desire for love and beauty come from?

Splitting the Difference

To answer these questions from the Vedic texts, a group of Masters appeared over many years, presenting a different final conclusion to our journey of learning. Shankara's monistic or "oneness with Brahman" view is called *advaita*, or nondistinctivism, because he proposed that the many atmas enter into Brahman and blend with it, no longer expressing their individuality or having forms.

The other Masters of Vedanta, most notably Ramanuja, Madhva, Nimbarka, Chaitanya, and Swami Narayan, agreed with Shankara that we are of the same nature as Brahman and then added that the Vedas clearly state that inside the Brahman there is another entirely Transcendental world of forms and beings.

They further said that once we enter Brahman, we (our atmas) have the option, the free will, to retain our distinctive individuality. We have what's called a Transcendental form, a kind of eternal-light body—and in that body, we continue to experience beauty and love for eternity. In this view, we and the Supreme Being, *Bhagavan*, interact in a sweet, loving relationship in the forests and meadows of eternity, within the space of Akshara Brahman.

The Sanskrit word *bhaga* means "six qualities or desirable things: wealth, strength, knowledge, beauty, fame, and renunciation" and combined with *van*, "one who possesses," produces the Vedic word for the Supreme Person and Being—God. That person who has the six bhagas to an unlimited degree is called *Bhagavan*. The companion word is *Krishna*, which means "most attractive" or that Being who "is so compellingly attractive that no one can resist."

You will often see these two words together as Bhagavan Krishna. This is the Vedic definition for the English God-Supreme Being, who in the Vedas is said to reside on Transcendental planets within the Akshara Brahman.

Therefore, where Shankara taught advaita Vedanta, these other Masters taught various versions of *dvaita* Vedanta. *Dvaita* means "distinctions"—not "dualism," as it has been so often translated—the idea being that upon our liberation and entrance into Brahman, we can, if we so choose, *continue as a distinctive individual* surrounded by eternal Divine beauty in the company of the Supreme Person, Bhagavan Krishna.

While yogis and professors may have a personal preference for one or the other view, it is clear that both views are present in the Vedas. The result is more freedom of choice even as we matriculate from the University of Matter, past the empty space of Nirvana, and on to the Eternal Light of Akshara Brahman. At that wondrous point, we can choose to either blend with Brahman in an eternal state of conscious bliss or we can enter one of the endless Transcendental planets, described by the Vedas as *Vaikuntha Loka*, or "the planets of eternal love where no one has any anxiety or fear." In this Loka, the many atmas who choose to do so exist inside the Akshara Brahman sky on a Vaikuntha planet and continue their individual existence with one another and the Supreme Being, Bhagavan, aka God.

If one adheres to this personal Transcendental view and makes this choice, then the Ultimate Reality is revealed as a personal loving Being named Shri Bhagavan Krishna. From this perspective, it is the Ultimate Transcendental Personal Divine who descends as the Ultimate Avatar we've been discussing. In this view, all the beauty we ever sought within matter (and couldn't attain), including our own truest personhood and the unconditional love of other beings, is eternally present within the Akshara Brahman and the many Vaikuntha Lokas.

If both Vedantic views are right, which the Vedas says is so, then it is we who may choose what we take from the Transcendental and how we live there. This is apparent when the Ultimate Avatars descend from this Akshara Brahman Vaikuntha abode. To one seeker of a certain nature, the Avatars are an appearance of the One Great Reality into which they wish to blend, to merge and enter as one. To another seeker, the Ultimate Avatar is the Person of the Divine, descending to Earth with an invitation to an eternal dance.

Great work following the three paths. Don't worry if it was excessively mind bending. I'll repeat the three scenarios, using a movie-projector metaphor that will help a lot in clarifying the subtle differences between Transcendental Nirvana, Brahman, and Vaikuntha Loka.

Scenario One: You are watching a movie (symbolizing all life as most of us see it—the material world). Being attracted to the material-world movie, as we all are, you run at the screen, trying to join in with the characters. Instead—boom!—you bump your face on the screen and get a bloody nose (birth, disease, old age, death). After doing this several times (many lifetimes—it's an epic), you give up and sit down next to the screen and begin instead to meditate upon all these images. You soon discover that the images are not what they appear to be (they are temporary) or even where they appear to be. They are clearly different from the screen. At this point, you realize you cannot join the movie (the movie is not you), and in your profound understanding, you become detached, transcendental, and achieve Nirvana.

Scenario Two: Next, out of the corner of your third eye, you notice that the images on the screen are actually coming down from the projector (the Creator, Brahma, and the Devas). As you follow this shining light back to its source, you are ascending through all the higher and subtler realms of matter (realms of the Devas). Higher and higher you go, until you finally reach the lens of the projector. Putting your eye right up to the lens, the screen and the forms (the images) instantly disappear in a blinding, joyful effulgence of golden light. You feel blissful. In basking in this light, you have achieved another form of transcendence: the Akshara Brahman, the positive but formless state of eternal, conscious, joyful existence.

Scenario Three: Somewhere in the golden light, you find yourself asking one final question: "But wait! If the golden light is truly formless, then how did the forms that appeared as the movie (realms of matter) arise from a formless Transcendental reality?" Fascinated, compelled, and enchanted, you continue even higher into the bliss, past the lens of the projector, and all the way into the projection room, where forms are again visible. Wow. Beyond that room, you can see that you can travel to the actual place where the movie (material world) was made (Vaikuntha Loka). There you meet the actors, the directors, the set and costume designers, and even the person who's behind all of it (the Supreme Being). And you're not getting autographs, you're dancing. And you realize how it all unfolds: the material world is a real but temporary reflection on a screen of matter of the projected eternal forms and beings who live in the realms of the Transcendental planets.

This transcendental party for the cast and crew (liberated atmas) is where the distinctivist Vedantins of the Transcendentalist path desire to go—beyond Nirvana, beyond the Brahman experience of pure oneness, and finally to Vaikuntha Loka, where all original and eternal beauty plays.

In Vaikuntha Loka, we meet the countless eternal beings and the Supreme Being, Bhagavan, and His eternal, inseparable Female counterpart. All of these Divine Transcendental beings have light bodies instead of the partially lit dark bodies of matter. Here, form and beauty, flowers, trees, the entire realm exist without birth, disease, old age, or death. This is Vaikuntha Loka, where all the original, eternal, beautiful Transcendental forms are the real world, reflected into the material world—where we are now a "photocopy" of the Transcendental realm.

These are the three Transcendental realms. All three are blissfully beyond anything we can experience here. According to the Avatars, we will go where we set our sights. We will go where we desire. You don't have to buckle up. You have to unbuckle.

A Summary of the Transcendental

In the Nirvana and Akshara Brahman views of liberation, we leave the material world behind and graduate to an empty or impersonal final state, which, while free of suffering, is without any of the beauty that attracted us within matter. In both the Nirvana and Brahman states, there are neither flowers nor individuals to smell them. Though these states are known to be joyful and free of suffering, they are also homogenized, more like the child in the womb, with no more individuality for the atma; no God, Bhagavan, or Supreme Being; and no forms of the beauty and desire that had originally attracted us to live within the realms of matter and are, after all, the driving force of matter.

Transcendentally Yours

Here on Earth, if we love someone and that person loves us, it is often the case that by consent we take liberties with them. In the Transcendental realm, there are no moral or dualistic conflicts, and everyone is liberated and free to play creatively. The reason for this harmonious and sublime interaction is that in the Transcendental realm, the Supreme Beings—both male and female, the Divine

Couple—known in part through millions of names spoken by their devotees in countless trillions of Universes, are personally visible and lovingly present at the center of all activities. All the residents can see, adore, serve, and freely communicate and interact with those Supreme Beings.

The word *supreme* is derived from two Sanskrit words that describe the highest state of Divine love and sweet service. *Su* means "a thousand times better" and *prema* is "the purest, most ecstatic, most sublime and delicious form of love exchanged between the Divine Couple" and the countless atmas. So for those liberated atmas who wish to participate, the Transcendental worlds *with form and distinctive individuality* allow them to finally and eternally fulfill and exchange the sweetest love to an unlimited degree—a love only hinted at through all our many loving experiences while in matter.

Hold the image of this kind of love in both your mind and heart. Consider that the Supreme Being, the Source of All—who as Big God has at times been described as almighty, angry, and judgmental—can actually appear to us in the loving form we desire. According to the yogis, this *Su-prema* Being will exchange love with us, as we desire. This is described as a *rasa* or "flavor" of love. *Prema* means "a thousand times greater than the greatest love."

The Avatars tell us there are various possible love flavors, related and similar to those we experience on Earth. Clearly, the flavors of love shared with a child, master, friend, parent, or even lover create very different emotions. In Vaikuntha—"the abode where there is no anxiety"—however, these forms of love can be experienced to an *unlimited* degree. The Vedas reveal that we can go to the Transcendental home of all, choose to go to the grandest of parties, and in the chambers of eternity, dance cheek to cheek with Bhagavan—the most amazing Person in all of existence. Earth is a sort of practice planet where we become the most loving person we can be. We graduate to the Transcendental abode of the Supreme Being when we know how to exchange varities of love and to serve in many Divine ways.

Welcome Home

The Vedic sages report that once we are freed of all matter and our limitations in the material world, at the moment of graduation, just after we leave our final material bodies, if we have chosen to enter the distinctive realms of Vaikuntha, we are transported to the boundary of that realm on the wings of a great flying ship. At the boundary of Vaikuntha is a great lake called Ara, in which we bathe. We then cross a beautiful river called Viraja. At the entrance to this realm, we are met by hundreds of joyful residents who welcome us with immortal garlands and feed us refreshing fruits from the Kalpa Vriksha trees, which yield any kind of fruit that is desired. We are then anointed with divine fragrance, dressed in beautiful robes, and led forward into a great hall where Bhagavan and Bhagavati, the Divine Couple, personally welcome us back and celebrate the conclusion of our epic journey from the realms of matter.

It is from this Transcendental realm that the Ultimate Avatars descend and have descended to reveal to us our true home—the Transcendental Akshara Brahman and the Vaikuntha planets of eternally creative, loving freedom. Knowledge of Vaikuntha, and countless other secrets, are revealed by the Avatars in the two great epics left behind on Earth during their last two visits. Those epics are called the *Ramayana* and the *Mahabharata*. That's where we're going next.

TWELVE

RAM AND SITA—
THE ETERNAL ROMANCE

Namaste, I see you glowing in the garden of your heart like Sita waiting for Ram, like Hanuman finding his power in sacred service, like Jatayu giving his life for truth. You are also in exile from your true nature, wandering the dark forests of matter, seeking a love that will never end.

Long, long ago when the Earth was still a young maiden, India—then known as Bharata—was a lush garden of primal forests and fragrant valleys. Cold had no power here, so fruits and food of all kinds and endless varieties of fragrant flowers grew in such abundance that no one was ever hungry. Noble sages wandered the forests without fear, meditating upon the Brahman and Bhagavan, the inconceivable infinite reality. Yogis lived in the forest to hold the balance of Mother Nature. They founded schools of deep learning beneath the sheltering branches of vast primordial banyan trees. These trees incorporated the constant chanting of Vedic hymns into their annual rings of growth, so that the very molecules of their being vibrated with the holy sound.

It was near the end of the second age. The cosmic clock had ticked to the Silver Age, past the Golden Age when everything was perfect. That silver was now wearing thin and getting ready to tarnish into the adversarial Bronze Age. Bad omens and signs of disturbance were beginning to appear in dark corners of the forest. Evil does not shout its presence boldly; being a coward, it whispers in the dark until the truth of dharma is undermined. Only then do the dark ones come out of hiding and remove their disguises.

The Coming Storm

In the Golden and Silver ages, the Devas and Devis of the higher realms were regularly *seen* on Bhumi. Their flashing flower airplanes, powered by pulses of sacred sound, were often spotted. Beautiful *Apsaras*, the sensual Divas of the Devas, were often startled at their bath as they luxuriated in the crystal waters of mountain streams. Though it was frowned upon by the Deva and human leaders, occasionally a yogi meditating deep in the forest or a noble prince and an Apsara of unimaginable beauty would embrace each other in a brief, irresistible tryst, a meeting between two worlds. The Devi would conceive and give birth to the child immediately and then return to its subtle abode. These semihuman Devas would often grow up to become extraordinary human beings.

Sometimes the Devas would also enlist earthly kings to assist them in their fight against the cosmic dark ones who always threatened harmony and balance in the worlds of matter. The Vedas show us that the realms of matter are always a mixture of dark and light, unlike the light's source in the Transcendental, where everything is conscious, joyful, effulgent existence. So within each of the countless trillion Universes, there is always a gradient of dark and light. The light is the domain of the Bright Ones—the Devas—whereas the dark is home of the Asuras, the dark ones, who oppose the light and all it stands for.

In the realms of matter, this oppositional dichotomy is always present. Sometimes the light drives away the dark, but sometimes the dark clouds of asuric chaos threaten all life. All the atmas who come to the material world are at risk of being enrolled into the Asuras' dark agenda. In the dark forest of matter, both good and evil could be waiting around any corner. Because humans have free will, they can chose either enlightenment or endarkenment—to join the Deva army or that of the Asuras—but fight they must!

Just as our bodies have helper cells and sometimes cancer cells, the epics tell us a malignant tumor was growing off the coast of India on the island we now call Sri Lanka. The Dark Lord at the center of this nest of festering evil was a yogi "gone bad" named Ravana. After achieving all the mystic powers and blessings of the Devas, Ravana had chosen the dark side for his personal aggrandizement. Intoxicated with his immense power, he began to practice the dark arts of enslaving others to his will. He became a cannibal in order to quickly absorb the powers of others. No one was safe from his terrible power. His body morphed under the impact of so much greed. He became a *rakshasa*, an "eater of the hearts of humans." He grew ten ferocious heads and, though still handsome, was distorted and deformed because of his many evil deeds. Raping beautiful women was one of his favorite pleasures, and he brought many to grief this way until one of his victims cursed him, saying that if he raped again, he would immediately die.

Everywhere Ravana went with his ten ravenous heads, people screamed with pain at his atrocities. Ravana appeared unstoppable, a monster temporarily protected by the grace of his previous ways of Yoga and austerities. Only two creatures were immune to his protective shield for, in his pride, he had forgotten to ask for immunity from lowly humans and animals, either of which could, because of this oversight, kill Ravana.

Undercover Atmas

A plot was unfolding beyond the understanding of Ravana or any Deva or human. The time had come for a descent to Earth by the great Avatar Bhagavan, the all-powerful, all-knowing, all-loving friend of all, who lives eternally visible in the luminous meadows of the realm of Brahman—in Vaikuntha, the joyful realm where there is no anxiety or fear. This was the historical right moment for a visit to Mother Earth to take place by the embodiment of dharma, truth, kindness, strength, protection, wisdom, and above all, the sweetest love. Bhagavan disguised himself as a human prince, Shri Ram, hidden but descending on a purposeful mission of mercy. Bhagavan took form and descended to Earth as a prince in the most noble royal family in India. His eternal female counterpart, Lakshmi, was also to be a pivotal part of this story. She took the form of Shri Sita Devi and was born into another great family as the daughter of the king Janaka.

Laughing at the thought of the great adventure they had planned, Bhagavan invited thousands of his friends and associates in Brahman to descend and take birth in key families and places. Then laughing even more, he instructed all the greatest Devas to take birth in the forests of India as apes and bears. Animals like no one had seen before or since were about to take birth and would soon become the unsuspecting nemeses of Ravana. The greatest of the Devas is Vayu, the wind. He had long prayed to Bhagavan for a special service. Bhagavan winked and fulfilled his wish, and the mighty Deva became Hanuman, the monkey general who would become the hero of the story. That is Bhagavan's way—he does everything in the background and gives credit to those he loves.

Shri Ram and Sita looked at each other and again laughed at the plan: Bhagavan (Ram) and his eternal consort (Sita) were about to take birth on Earth as the perfect royal couple. Ravana had no idea of the plot he was in the middle of, but Bhagavan and friends were about to avatar, to descend and rescue the Earth from evil, bless the innocent, and get up to some epic monkey business in the process.

However, this was no everyday garden-variety Avatar of a Deva or brilliant Divine—this was to be the descent of the *purna* Avatar, the full manifestation of Bhagavan's divinity. The circus was about to come to town on Indian soil, and not just any show but what we might call the Cirque du "Soul." Since that time, this amazing story has been called the *Ramayana* as recorded by the great yogi/sage Valmiki. He is the greatest poet to ever to walk the Earth. The twenty-four thousand Sanskrit verses of this great poem contain *all* of the Avatar teachings. I am merely a firefly in his service—as are these few words, morsels from the table of that great Divine feast.

When Shri Ram appeared as the son of King Dasaratha, the court astrologers were ecstatic. They had never seen such a horoscope. Every planet was brilliant, every omen auspicious. No human could have such a chart. "Could it be?" they thought. "Dare we say?" They did. This would be the greatest king ever to walk the Earth, dharma personified, a great warrior, always kind, truthful in every matter, compassionate. But then the astrologers hesitated at what they saw in the chart. His marriage would be ... difficult ... no, not difficult ... an epic story.

No one had ever seen such a beautiful baby as Ramachandra, as he was called. And eventually his three brothers, Bharat, Lakshman, and Shatrughna, were the joy of King Dasaratha, as were his three wives and their mothers. Everyone adored Ram in ways they could not fully understand. They loved him more than their own lives, as if the very source of their lives was before them in human form. The same was true of Sita. Her beauty, charm, wisdom, depth, and artistry were beyond anyone's understanding or ability to measure. The Source of all, the inscrutable eternal and unlimited Reality, was purposely "hiding" inside human bodies to play a game on Earth for the good of all. Some knew who they were, some did not; it is always this way because, as the Vedas show us, Bhagavan loves us as we love

Bhagavan. This is an eternal game of hide-and-seek where we are in charge, except that we've forgotten. It appears as if everything is run by impersonal or despotic power, so we think we are lost. But in fact, the greatest force is love, which can never be forced upon another. We must cry for it, hunger for it, and give all for it. Try to imagine Ram's mother, Kausalaya, and how she must have felt breast feeding the Source of All. Mad, yes—love is always a bit mad. Ram was there on terra firma to give everyone a vision of his beauty. For friends, it would bring the greatest joy; for Ravana—well, wait a moment and see.

Dasharatha, Shri Ram's noble father, was a great king; his capital was Ayodhya, a city of immense beauty and peace. No one went hungry, there was no crime, and sparkling streets were cleaned and perfumed every morning. Happy citizens respected one another, and one celebration or another was always beautifying the holy city. Gold was everywhere, jewels decorated the houses, and bright birds sang joyful songs and flashed their colored wings everywhere. Sparkling ponds burst with pink lotuses, and graceful swans played in their stems. It was real—such care and trust in the eye of every neighbor. It makes me cry to remember that once life was like this. And when Ram was there, it was a thousand times brighter.

Dark Clouds

All was peaceful until one day, when the evil that had been distant came to call. Vishvamitra, head of all the forest-dwelling sages, came to Ayodhya and, with a concerned look upon his face, bowed before the king. By this time, Shri Ram was a handsome sixteen-year-old. His younger brother, Lakshman, and he were inseparable. As princes, they had been well educated and trained in all the royal arts, and they were skilled with bows and arrows and all weapons. Their handsome and noble features inspired everyone who saw them. Vishvamitra stood in front of King Dasharatha and delivered his stunning message: that the

Asuras from Lanka had begun a series of raids upon the forest-dwelling yogis, destroying altars and sacred areas and killing milk cows and destroying crops. These dark raiders from Ravana's camp were becoming bolder. The problem had become critical, and an immediate response was needed.

Though elderly by this time—a fact Ravana and his men were counting on—the courageous Dasharatha said he would immediately prepare to go to the forest at the head of an army. To Dasharatha's surprise, Vishvamitra insisted instead that Ram and Lakshman accompany him to the forest to fight the Asuras. Because of his intense love for Ram, King Dasaratha, and indeed all the court who loved Ram so, was horrified to think of the young prince facing evil and dangerous Asuras in battle. But the great sage Vishvamitra, who could see past, present, and future, assured the king that only Ram and his brother could fulfill this destiny. The king's spiritual adviser, Vasistha, agreed with Vishvamitra.

As the two brothers left Ayodhya, the plot of this Divine story starts to pick up speed. As they traveled through the forest, Vishvamitra began the princes' initiation into the advanced martial arts that combine powerful mantras with ordinary weapons. Through these ancient, closely guarded secrets, ultimate weapons that harness the great forces of Nature were taught to the noble protectors of society. These weapons were necessary to withstand and overcome the terrible powers of the dark beings. Light drives away dark. However, in this world there is always more dark.

Once the nobles reached the monastery, deep in the forest, the evil Asuras soon appeared. To them nothing was sacred. They enjoyed desecrating sacred altars, raping any women they found, and killing and eating their most tender victims. The cancer was spreading. But this was only a small raiding party, and the evil ones were not expecting the two Divine brothers to be deep in the forest. Testing their new mantra-powered *astras*, the brothers easily defeated the intruders, killing several and forcing the rest back to Lanka to report that they had been repulsed. The war was on, and rumblings were heard in the distance.

The Wedding Bow

When the time came for Ram and Lakshman to return to Ayodhya, Vishvamitra, with a knowing twinkle in his eye, suggested that they visit the nearby realm of the famous King Janaka, who was known throughout India for his nobility. Sita, rumored to be the most refined and beautiful princess anyone had ever seen, was now old enough to marry. The story goes that Sita was born directly from the Earth. The king was plowing the earth with a golden plow in a sacred ceremony for abundance, when Sita appeared from the ground he had just touched.

In Janaka's palace, there was a bow so great it took five hundred strong men just to move it. The king had announced that anyone who could string the bow could also marry Sita. When Ram, Lakshman, and Vishvamitra arrived, the bow was on display. Ram went up to it, picked it up easily, strung it, bent it into a circle, and then with a roar, to everyone's amazement, the bow snapped in two. It was not long thereafter that Ram and Sita had a chance meeting in the palace garden. One look was all they needed to know. Each silently vowed that the other was the only love. Soon thereafter, they were standing together in front of the sacred fire reciting the holy vows of a lifetime commitment to each other. Bhagavan and his eternal beloved consort were again united in a marriage that would change the course of history. The English word *romantic* is derived from the Sanskrit word *Ram*, and Shri Ram saw only one thing when he closed his eyes: Sita Devi. As for Sita, she vowed, "Without your love, surely I will die."

The Doubts That Destroy

When Ram and Sita returned to Ayodhya, plans were already in motion to crown Ram as the regent. His elderly father wished to see Ram upon the throne. But like a cobra in a nursery, Ravana had reached a tentacle of his evil inside the king's palace. Dasaratha's youngest and favorite wife was the beautiful Kaikeyi. Her son was Bharata, the noble brother of Ram, and the unseen snake was Manthara, the evil and hunchbacked personal handmaiden of Kaikeyi. While Bharata was traveling, Manthara invented a story that Ram was planning to kill Bharata and that Kaikeyi needed to act quickly to secure her own rights by sending Ram into exile and having Bharata installed as king instead. Manthara's evil words overtook Kaikeyi's heart. Because Kaikeyi once saved Dasaratha's life, Dasaratha owed her a *boon* (favor), which he promised she could have at any time. He never imagined she would use it in such a terrible way. Under the evil influence of Ravana's poisonous treachery, Kaikeyi went to Dasaratha and asked that Prince Ram be sent into exile for fourteen years and that her son Bharata be made king.

Immediately the peaceful kingdom was torn by strife. Dasaratha loved Ram, but he had given his word to Kaikeyi, who now was adamant that nothing else would satisfy her. The long-standing tradition of Vedic kings was to be bound by their word of honor. Though it broke his heart and he would die soon after Ram went into exile, Dasaratha was powerless. He called his beloved eldest son to him, explained the terrible situation, and teary, ordered Ram to the forest for fourteen years of exile. Ram immediately grasped that the fate of Ayodhya now rested in his hands. By right, he could assert his claim as regent or use force, as he was loved by all. But if he did so, his father's honor would be betrayed, his family fragmented, and all things he held dear would be brought to ruin. The poison of Ravana now threatened everything.

Shri Ram bowed to his father, touched his aged feet with affection, and reassured him that all would be well. Ram knew that he could not lose his joy or calm in the midst of this threat to truth and goodness. He vowed that his brother Bharata would become king in his place, and he spoke sweetly to all who were angered or offended. Ram stopped all divisive thoughts, reminding everyone that this must be arranged by Divine plan.

Ram's brother Lakshman, with resolution that could not be shaken, swore he would join his brother in exile. Never, he said, would he leave Ram's side for any reason. Then Ram went before his beloved Sita, the tender and most beautiful flower of womanhood and the love of his life and heart. He touched her tenderly and told her of his exile to the fierce jungle for fourteen years and asked her to stay in Ayodhya where she would be safe and to remember him every day.

With tears in her eyes but in a clear and powerful voice, Sita replied to Ram that no fear, challenge, austerity, or danger could ever move her one inch from the side of her beloved husband and life partner. She reminded him that as a warrior, there was no situation that could arise in the jungle in which he could not protect her. She finally said to him that as long as his shadow was connected to his body, she would be at his side. And so Ram understood, and he and Lakshman and Sita prepared to leave Ayodhya on foot. Just before leaving, Ram had Sita distribute all their wealth to those in need. Shortly after Ram's departure, King Dasaratha died of a broken heart.

Exile in the Forest

Ayodhya was now without a king, so Bharata was sent for, and only then did he learn the truth of his mother's terrible actions. Angry at his mother but even more concerned for his beloved Ram, Bharata sped to where Ram was in the forest. He bowed to his brother and, in tears, asked for his sandals. Placing them on his head, he vowed that until Ram's exile was over, only Ram's sandals would sit on the throne of Ayodhya. They embraced, and Bharata returned to the city while Ram, Lakshman, and Sita proceeded deep into the forests of Dandaka.

It was a forest famous for its towering banyan trees, hundreds of feet tall, and the many ashrams of forest-dwelling yogis and *rishis*, as well as evil *rakshasas* who would hide in the dark caves. They posed as monks, but they were actually fierce and evil cannibals and practitioners of the black arts. With Ravana's power growing, the once-sacred and peaceful jungle, where yogis lived in peace with the wild beasts, was now a treacherous and uncertain place. One day as they walked around a bend, they saw a huge vulture perched in the tree above them. The brothers drew their bows, thinking this might be a shapeshifting asura. Instead, the bird spoke, introducing himself as one of Dasaratha's oldest friends. His name was Jatayu, and he volunteered to travel with them and guard Sita while Ram and Lakshman hunted. So their party grew to four.

A Blessing in Disguise

Along the way, the travelers visited many forest ashrams, where, when seeing the Divine Couple Shri Ram and Sita Devi paying them a personal visit, yogis realized the fulfillment of their long meditations. This is one of the reasons why the Avatars descended to make direct contact with those who had long loved them and prayed for a personal vision of their beauty. In lovely ways and with loving words, the Divine Father and Mother benedicted and blessed all wherever they went.

Finally, they arrived at a special spot in the Panchavati forest, which the sages had recommended. Sweet water flowed nearby, and flowers and fruits hung from fragrant trees. It was a paradise in the center of the mighty forest. There, Lakshman built a cottage, which was to be their home in exile. Cleverly constructed of earth, stones, and bamboo, it was a lovely forest retreat. Perhaps, they thought, a forest life could be peaceful after all.

Deceit Brings Destruction

But the wheel was turning faster. One day, while the three sat talking near their home, Ravana's sister Surpanaka wandered upon their cottage. She was an ugly and fearsome cannibal, but seeing the handsome prince, she assumed a beautiful human form. Swaying into their midst, she began to flirt, first with Ram and then with Lakshman. Finally growing impatient, she rushed at Sita to destroy her. Lakshman interceded and quickly cut off Surpanaka's ears and nose with his sword. She flew screaming in pain across the forest to where her other brother Khara was camped with a large army of marching rakshasas. Hearing his sister's story and seeing her wounds, this horrific general of evil forces led his army to the area around Panchavati. When Ram saw the Asuras, he asked Lakshman to guard Sita and stood before the dark army twanging his bow. Once the fight began, blood was flowing everywhere, but none of it was Ram's. Sixteen thousand maneaters were soon destroyed, then the officers, and finally the wicked Khara himself lay dying on the bloodstained ground. Only one soldier escaped to carry this story of defeat to Ravana.

The Avatar had begun his other mission: ridding Mother Bhumi of the cancer cells in demon form who were harming all life. Meanwhile, an apparent mere mortal had challenged the mighty Ravana, whose power frightened even the Devas. The reaction of Ravana was fury, the likes of which had never been seen.

Retaliation—the Kidnapping of Sita

Ravana's first impulse was to launch an immediate direct attack. He would crush this puny human insect and be done with him in a moment. However, the disfigured and angry Surpanaka wanted revenge. She knew her brother's weakness was beautiful women. So Surpanaka told Ravana of Sita's unsurpassed beauty and suggested he kidnap her and have his revenge by ravishing her for his pleasure. Ravana hatched a plan: his henchman Maricha would take the form of a jewel-encrusted magical deer and appear before Sita as a distraction. The plan worked. Ram chased after the alluring deer, who then imitated Ram's voice calling for help. Lakshman ran after Ram, leaving Sita alone. Before Lakshman left, he drew a magic circle around the cottage, saying she would be safe within that boundary. At that moment Ravana appeared, dressed in the orange robes of a holy man and begged Sita for water. Overwhelmed by compassion, she offered water to the disguised asura, and in so doing, her hand reached outside the circle. In a moment, she was yanked out and thrown roughly into Ravana's chariot, which rose up in the sky and began to fly away.

Out of nowhere, the loyal vulture Jatayu attacked the chariot, screaming and tearing at Ravana's flesh. But even with the advantage of surprise, Jatayu was no match for Ravana, who soon cut off both of the vulture's wings and with a sneer sent Jatayu crashing to the ground. Then, laughing at his success, Ravana flew toward the ocean on the way to his stronghold on Sri Lanka. Just as they were about to cross the ocean, the resourceful Sita wrapped her ornaments in a piece of her sari. She threw them to the ground in the hopes that someone might find them. Indeed, the ornaments landed near five large monkeys.

Arriving at his capital city made entirely of gold, Ravana placed the grief-stricken Sita in the wooded Ashoka Garden surrounded by female guards. Once Sita was his prisoner and securely guarded, Ravana approached her. He had never seen such beauty in any woman. Even among his queen, Mandodari, and the thousands of beauties in his harem, none was close to the infinite beauty of Sita Devi. After all, she was the Divine Feminine who had descended to Earth. Bewildered, Ravana approached Sita like a lover courting a young maiden. He promised her all pleasures and wealth and reminded her that the puny mortal Ram was unable to please her as he certainly could. Finally, Sita replied in words that stung Ravana like a nest of wasps. She chastised him in a hundred ways, warning him that Ram would kill him for kidnapping her. Finally she told him, "The consort of a noble swan will not even look at an ugly, garbage-eating crow." His eyes red with anger, Ravana replied that if Sita did not agree to be his wife within twelve months, then she would be his breakfast instead. With these words, he left, leaving Sita surrounded by evil guards.

Brother in Arms

Meanwhile, in the Panchavati forest, both Ram and Lakshman hurried back to the cottage only to discover they were too late. Ram was desperate with anxiety and grief. Sita was gone without a trace. With tears in their eyes and heavy hearts, Ram and Lakshman searched everywhere in the forest in widening circles, desperately looking for a sign of Sita. Near the end of the day, as the deep red Sun was setting, they saw the mangled and bloody body of Jatayu. At first Ram thought it was a rakshasa covered in Sita's blood, so he fixed a deadly shaft to his bow. But then the sad and weakened voice of the dying Jatayu called out, "Ram! Ram! Ram!" Ram and Lakshman rushed to his side. Ram embraced his broken and bleeding body. Crying with his last breath, the loyal Jatayu told Ram the story of how he fought Ravana, had his wings severed, and saw Sita carried away. As the Sun set, Jatayu left his body while looking into Ram's face. Lakshman and Ram gave him a funeral of the highest honor. The following day Ram and Lakshman began their desperate search for Sita.

The Search for Sita

It was the spring of their thirteenth year of exile when Ram and Lakshman finally reached Rishyamukha Mountain. Without Ram's beloved Sita, the fragrant flowers and creatures in their ecstatic frenzy of mating and renewed life only drove Ram deeper into depression. Lakshman had no words that could give Ram solace. The brothers had heard of a humanlike race of apes whose king was named Sugriva. The sages had told them that only the great apes and bears would be capable of searching everywhere for Sita. But as fate would have it, Sugriva's cruel brother Vali had stolen his wife Tara and usurped his throne. Sugriva was now living in exhile on Rishyamukha Mountain with his loyal followers and his prime minister, the inimitable Hanuman.

If you recall from the beginning of our story, due to Ravana's own pride, he could only be killed by humans or animals—nothing *greater*. So the Supreme Being instructed the Devas to take birth as monkeys and bears, the most remarkable of whom would be Hanuman, the Avatar of Vayu, the Deva of the wind and air.

When Ram told the monkeys the sad story of Sita's abduction, they chattered among themselves for some time until Sugriva told Ram and Lakshman that five of their kind had seen a beautiful princess being abducted earlier in the year and that she had thrown down to the ground some jewelry wrapped in a piece of her sari. They brought this to Ram and, to his delight, he discovered they were Sita's. This was the first sign that they were on the trail of finding Princess Sita, and there was hope that these monkeys could help in the search. But first, Sugriva needed help with his problem.

The bears and monkeys were still asleep to their Divine nature and purpose for being on Earth, but that was soon to be reawakened. Sugriva sent Hanuman to meet Ram and Lakshman. In spite of his monkey body, Hanuman spoke perfect Sanskrit and had mastered the Vedas and the art of diplomacy. When he introduced himself to Ram and Lakshman, they were astounded at Hanuman's eloquence and knowledge. Hanuman, on the other hand, knew immediately that serving the Supreme Lord Ram was his forgotten destiny. Over the next few months, Ram and Lakshman launched a campaign against Vali—King Sugriva's cruel brother who had stolen Sugriva's wife and usurped his throne. Ram finally killed Vali, and Sugriva's wife Tara was returned to him. Now it was Sugriva's turn to help Ram. Sugriva called to all the monkeys, for hundreds of miles around, instructing them to come to him within ten days.

Within two weeks, a host of monkeys and bears had assembled. Millions of monkeys of every size and shape, along with hosts of great bears, strategically camped throughout the forest. They were divided into four groups, each group searching in one of the four directions. Hanuman's group was to go south. Before Hanuman left, though, Shri Ram called him to his side. He told Hanuman that he was placing the most trust in him and so removed his royal signet ring and gave it to Hanuman, saying Sita would only believe Ram had sent Hanuman if she saw Ram's personal ring.

After a while, Hanuman's group of monkeys and bears reached the sea. Above them a large vulture, so old it had no feathers, emerged from a cave where he lived. This was Sampati, the older brother of Jatayu, that brave vulture who had died defending Sita. With his extraordinary vision, Sampati pointed the monkey search party across the ocean to Ravana's island. She is there, he told them, but someone must leap across the ocean—unless they can fly!

The monkeys looked at one another in confusion until one among them stepped forward. It was Hanuman. Something impossible was about to happen.

Leap of Faith

The veil that had allowed mighty Devas to unconsciously play as earthly monkeys was giving way. The dark thoughts of what they could not do were about to be chased away by the rising Sun of service to the Supreme Beings. Hanuman was the first to feel this as he held Ram's ring in his hand and thought of Sita being held in prison. Within Hanuman, something profound had changed: he remembered his true nature. He was—no, he *is* Vayu—Deva of the wind, servant of Ram, rescuer of Sita. Hanuman's body began to grow, to expand. He dug his toes into the earth—and the earth began to tremble as he chanted "Ram, Ram, Ram"—and then with a mighty roar he leapt, flying many miles over the vast ocean, on, on, on, until finally he landed on the other shore in Lanka. Hanuman was now on the verge of confronting the mighty and impenetrable Ravana on the demon's own soil and to try to encourage Sita and finally bring good news back to Ram. From that point on, nothing was impossible for the mighty Hanuman.

But with no clues, Hanuman first had to search throughout the vast Golden City to find Sita. Shrinking himself to a tiny form, he quietly slipped under the city gates. There he found his way to Ravana's mighty palace, which rose up like a mountain of gold. It had facilities for enjoying every conceivable pleasure, drinking rooms, a vast harem of beautiful women, and fierce rakshasas guarding every gate and door.

Although the time was hundreds of thousands of years before today, Hanuman discovered, in one large room, Ravana's personal aircraft made of gold and jewels, hovering above the floor as if poised for flight. After relentless searching, Hanuman found the Ashoka Grove in which Sita was being held prisoner. In the middle of that grove was a large, pure white pagoda with a thousand grand pillars. Its steps were made of coral and its platform of gold. On that platform Sita sat dressed in a dirty, gold sari, lean and emaciated, with tears streaming down her cheeks. Quietly Hanuman climbed the nearby tree, which spread itself over Sita.

Hanuman drew close and finally began to speak to Sita. At first she thought he was an asura, but when he gave her Ram's ring, she believed who he said he was, and in return she gave him an ornament that she had always worn in her hair. Hanuman offered to carry Sita back to Ram immediately, but she reminded him that only Ram could hold her body next to his.

This was the tenth month of Sita's captivity, and time was running out, so Hanuman had to act quickly. Still, just before he left, he decided to cause some trouble in Ravana's palace. He leapt on the roof and began destroying everything in his path. Like angry hornets, the rakshasa soldiers rushed at Hanuman, but Hanuman killed many of them until he was finally overcome by a magic weapon. Bound hand and foot, Hanuman was brought before King Ravana. Hanuman brazenly warned Ravana of his impending death at Ram's hands and demanded Sita's release. Mocking the fearless monkey, Ravana had Hanuman's tail lit on fire. But as a farewell gesture, Hanuman broke free from his bonds and with his tail flaming, jumped from building to building burning everything in sight. Then with a mighty roar he again assumed his gigantic form and leapt back across the waters to his beloved Shri Ram.

Moving Mountains

Upon his return, Hanuman informed Ram of Sita's whereabouts, and Ram, with tears in his eyes, received Sita's hairpin. They made a plan to build a bridge of stones between India and Sri Lanka. Once the monkey and bear army assembled, Ram wrote his name on huge rocks, which then floated on the water's surface. Upon these floating rocks, the crew built the bridge to Lanka. Ravana was surprised how quickly the forces reached his stronghold and were at his doorstep, how fierce those he once brushed aside as the insignificant—animals and puny humans. And so the Great War began.

The epic battle raged for weeks, Ravana's brother Kumbhakarna, a gigantic cannibal, was sent into battle, killing many monkeys and bears. Finally he was destroyed. Then Indrajit, Ravana's evil and magical son, fought and killed many of the monkeys and bears, but eventually he, too, was destroyed, along with millions of Ravana's rakshasa soldiers. In one of the darkest moments of the battles, both Ram and Lakshman were hit by poison arrows and soon lay dying on the ground. A heroic Hanuman immediately flew to a nearby mountain famous for the herb that could heal them. The rakshasas had already set it on fire to prevent the medicine from reaching Ram and Lakshman, so Hanuman picked up the entire mountain and brought it back. The herb was found and saved from the flames, and Ram and Lakshman revived.

Ravenously Yours

The final battle, of course, was between Bhagavan Shri Ram and Ravana. In the material world, those who are good allow themselves to be restrained by truth and dharma, so their power never exceeds certain limits. However, when those guidelines of behavior for the good *of all* are removed, a human can become a monster so powerful and dangerous that even the Devas—the personified laws of Mother Nature—are powerless to stop them. And when we humans violate those laws in ways that endanger all life, the Supreme Being comes as the full or Ultimate Avatar. For the gentle humans, the Avatar reveals the full potential of truth and love.

For the humans like Ravana, who choose to abuse their powers, the Avatar comes as Death personified. The Vedas show us that Death is either a cat with a kitten in its mouth or a cat with a rat in its mouth—we choose the relationship. The final confrontation between Shri Ram and the mighty Ravana ended with Ram shooting a blazing golden arrow while chanting a famous mantra to the Sun, the *Aditya Hridayam*.

The arrow struck Ravana in the heart, and he fell to the ground. As he lay there dying and his atma prepared to leave the body, some monkeys began to mock Ravana. Ram stopped them and said, "In spite of Ravana choosing the wrong path, he was a great hero."

The struggle was over. Sita was rescued and, for the moment, balance was restored to the Earth again. Because the Supreme Lord Ram killed Ravana personally, Ravana was purified for all his past evil deeds. After all, at a higher level of understanding, this entire drama was written and enacted by the Supreme Being for everyone's benefit, and Ravana was the lead actor—an eternal atma in a school play at the University.

Dharma Restored

The story is almost complete. Ram and Sita, the Divine Truth of Brahman incarnate *or* the Divine Couple from Vaikuntha Loka—according to your final choice of understanding—had appeared on Earth for one more reason. Together, as king and queen, they embody all the highest values and honorable behavior of the dharma of any noble ruler. They also embody the protection of family and tradition, care for elders, honor of wise rishis and sages, love of all citizens including all other beings and all life and, finally, sacred love between committed partners. These values have been cherished in India and across the world for many thousands of years—and their roots reach deeply into the story of Shri Ram and Sita Devi. As a king and queen, they had to prove one more thing to still the voices that doubted that loyalty and chastity between a man and woman are possible.

After Ram rescued Sita, you might have expected them to fall into each other's arms, as an everyday couple would, but they were the Ultimate Avatars, the Male and Female Divine, and the most celebrated royals in the world of their time. In any situation where an evil and charismatic person like Ravana violates the sanctity of the female through kidnapping and rape, the common people and gossipmongers would always expect disloyalty. So when Sita came before Ram, Ram spoke to her as if her virtue could be in doubt. As a queen, she understood and immediately asked Lakshman to build a large fire. Without hesitation, she walked into the flames saying, "If I have been untrue to you, I will give up my body." Immediately, the Deva of fire, Agni, appeared from within the flames and carried Sita unharmed from their midst. Only then was their reunion complete. Now no one could doubt the couple's love or purity.

Finally, the airplane that had belonged to Ravana was summoned. Shri Ram, Sita Devi, and Lakshman went onboard and began their return flight to Ayodhya, where for fourteen years Bharata had waited patiently for his brother's return and his coronation as the rightful king. Hanuman had gone ahead to inform Bharata of Ram's and Sita's imminent arrival. Bharata made all the arrangements for their coronation as king and queen. As Shri Ram and Sita Devi reentered Ayodhya, the lamps in every home lit of their own accord. Peace was restored, and the light of Divine wisdom shined in every home. At the coronation of Ram and Sita, with Lakshman standing near, Hanuman, the embodiment of pure truth, dharma, and devotion, came forward and knelt before Ram and Sita. Mother Sita, the Mother of All, reached down and placed a necklace of pearls over Hanuman's head—a symbol of his courage and devotion. The entire palace rang with shouts of joy: "Jai! Jai! Sita Ram! Victory to the Supreme Couple—may all believe in Eternal Love!"

epic love—ultimate avatar

*Namaste, I see you as a great hero on an epic journey, trying to decide what is
real and what is an illusion, seeking immortality in a world of chaos,
longing for the light in storms and darkness. I see you endure the
complex plots of those who no longer care. I see you find
the final joy and dance embracing the Love Supreme.*

According to the Vedas, the Ramayana took place 1.2 million years ago, a brief moment ago in cosmic time. Our modern notion of time has been circumscribed by three basic opinions. First, when Christians came to India in the 1600s, they believed that the Universe was created as we see it six thousand years ago and with an imminent end in the very near future. Second, and conversely, modern science has mostly promoted an evolutionary view of billions of years, with no Divine intervention of intelligence. Third, most Western historians start reckoning modern and scientific thought with Greek culture starting at about 500 BCE.

The Vedas reveal a much different story in which all existence ultimately, has neither a beginning or an end, and is pervaded and sustained by purposeful Divine Intelligence, while at the same time is evolving and changing form over stunningly long cycles—trillions of years—known as yugas.

Each of these views is a story that cannot be ultimately proven. There is some evidence but not enough for conclusiveness. For that reason, the Vedas show us that we will hear a version and accept or not accept it, as we individually choose. Nevertheless, whichever view of time and creation we pick, it will act as the context for all that we do. Whether we hold to reincarnation or an "only one life" view, how we live and the goals we set, as well as how we see others, will be affected by our view of time.

Just as we experience seasons in the course of a year, or seasons in life from childhood to old age, so the Vedas show that the cosmos passes through ages—ages that act like seasons of cosmic time. There is, in a sense, a spring, summer, fall, and winter, cosmically. The Vedic "year" is 4,320,000 of the Western world's years in length. Spring, summer, fall, and winter are the Golden, Silver, Bronze, and Iron seasons or ages, which are, respectively, 1,728,000 years, 1,296,000 years, 864,000 years, and 432,000 years in duration.

Cosmic Winter Begins

Approximately 5,200 years ago, we were poised at the entry point of the Iron Age, the beginning of cosmic winter. In Sanskrit, that age is called *Kali*, which meant a time of less clarity, the so-called age of quarrel or age of opinion.

Our story of the last full descent of the Avatar places the event in India at the juncture between the Bronze Age and the Iron Age. In one section of the *Mahabharata*, there are 125 astronomical references to the exact position of the planets at that time. Using computers, we can now validate that 5,200 or so years ago, according to those astronomical references, that precise moment took place.

So wind your clocks back further than usual as we replay the most recent descent of the full Avatar in India, at the beginning of cosmic winter, the extraordinary beginning of this age called Kali *Yuga*.

Of course, for many reasons, the sages of India were worried about the coming of cosmic winter. For countless generations, the Vedic Library of Spiritual and Material Knowledge was passed as an oral tradition, carefully memorized via the remarkably precise Sanskrit language. With Kali Yuga—the age of quarrel—the clarity of this transmission, the sages knew, was in jeopardy. They gathered and decided that this new age could deeply fragment their cooperative society. Specifically, crucial Avatar teachings would be lost—as would happen to countless Indigenous cultures in the next five thousand years. Therefore, it was decided that the entire library would be compiled in written form. India, in particular over the last thousand years of invasion and colonization, would also be deeply threatened by this historical tsunami, but since her ancient texts were written in the perfect Sanskrit language—and for this reason only—India would remain the most intact Indigenous culture. Indeed, because their stories were written down, I am still able to share them with you as they have been told for aeons.

One other momentous scenario was unknown to the diligent and farsighted yogis and rishis writing down the Vedas at the time. The Supreme Being Shri Krishna had decided to avatar on planet Earth—our Mother Bhumi—exactly before the changing of the age. The Avatar, as Shri Krishna, came to make a personal revelation of even greater magnitude than that of Shri Ram. Incidentally, one of the meanings for *Shri* in Sanskrit is "beautiful." It is also an honorific. The word Krishna means "the most attractive."

As mentioned earlier, the *Ramayana* is a single poem of twenty-four thousand Sanskrit verses. My brief telling of its core story in the previous chapter was not even a complete outline of the main characters and story points. By contrast, the *Mahabharata* is a massive one hundred thousand verses. The *Mahabharata* is not only a recounting of events from five thousand years ago; it is a history of India over thousands of years prior to Shri Krishna's birth.

For reasons of time and space, in this chapter I will only share scenes and glimpses of that great epic and hope that you will be inspired to read the full version. By the way, at the center of the *Mahabharata* is the *Bhagavad Gita*, the most famous philosophical explanation of the Vedas. The *Gita*, as it is often called, summarizes the core teachings of Bhagavan Shri Krishna in seven hundred remarkable verses and has been an inspiration to many great thinkers of our time, including Mahatma Gandhi, Albert Einstein, and Henry David Thoreau.

Every Avatar Has a Mission

Every Avatar, at the time of descent, has a mission related to the Earth's specific problems at the time. In addition, each has a theme that includes the revelation of certain Transcendental knowledge. In the case of Ram and Sita, they came as both an ideal monogamous royal couple and as the personifications of dharma and nobility. The Avatar of Bhagavan Shri Krishna had a very different flavor. His appearance is sometimes divided into three categories: intimate Krishna, political Krishna, and philosophical Krishna. From his birth to age eleven, Krishna revealed levels of relationship, playfulness, and intimacy that were beyond anything revealed previously. In his political role, He stood as the Supreme Diplomat, poised between the two eternal groups of humans in conflict. Finally, as the Ultimate Philosopher, He spoke the immortal verses of the *Bhagavad Gita*, which is the very core of Vedic teaching, and to this day the most concise and explicit statement of the eternal Truth yet received by humans.

Our story begins with the inscrutable thoughts of Bhagavan Shri Krishna, deep in the eternal forest of his Transcendental abode where he sat in the sweet company of Lakshmi, his consort and inseparable feminine counterpart.

The two knew the cosmic winter was coming and they wanted to reveal on Earth the nurturing provisions of divine wisdom that would feed and protect everyone during the long and difficult times to come. So not unlike a filmmaker whose life work culminates in a film greater than any ever before made, the Supreme Couple decided to avatar to Earth and leave behind their most profound teachings and secrets in a Divine epic of such magnitude that it would never be forgotten.

In preparation for their visit, they instructed the Devas of our Universe to take birth in royal families across India. A cast of thousands of perfected yogis were also invited to join in the drama as divine helpers. Both sides, the good and those who opposed them, were chosen to facilitate the evolutions in the University. An epic cast of players was necessary because Bhagavan Shri Krishna was setting the stage for the ultimate novel in which every character would have layers of meaning.

The *Mahabharata* is not only a historical account of the times; it is a psychological masterpiece, thriller, and mystery written by the Supreme Genius. In this epic, all the human psychological archetypes are cataloged, from the very best and most dharmic, to the most despicable, devious, and distorted. As the writer, producer, director, and cinematographer, Bhagavan was now ready to also be the main actor disguised as a human. He and his band of eternal companions began the great descent to Bhumi—Mother Earth—to once again restore the balance of the planet, protect the innocent, and reveal the inconceivable secrets of the Transcendental realm to those who were ready to hear. It would be lights, camera, action, Ultimate Avatar!

Asuras in Royal Dress

Just before Shri Krishna's appearance on Earth, the political situation in India had become intolerably dire. Most kings were corrupt, hiding behind their power and royal dress. Many good nobles had been driven into exile. The kidnapping of young women was on the rise. Dangerous armies of cruel men were everywhere, creating a mood of fear via extortion and an increased burdening of the taxpayers.

Mother Bhumi was groaning under their calloused feet and feeling grief for her suffering children. She had asked for help, praying the Avatar would come. There was indeed even a rumor that the Avatar was coming and would kill a particularly evil king called Kamsa, who was the brother of Krishna's soon-to-be-mother, Devaki.

Devaki and her husband, Vasudeva, had been confined to Kamsa's dungeon ever since Kamsa had heard the prophecy that their eighth child, a boy, would kill him. As a precaution, he had imprisoned them and then killed six of their newborn children in succession. The seventh child was mysteriously transferred out of Devaki's womb, and appeared to everyone as a miscarriage. That child was in fact soon born from the womb of another woman in a nearby rural community. The child, Balarama, would be known as Krishna's older brother.

Finally, Shri Krishna entered Devaki's womb.

When the time came, Shri Krishna appeared standing and effulgent in his Bhagavan form and told his parents that the Supreme Being had just appeared as their baby son. He then instructed his father to take him to the same rural community where his brother Balarama had gone. Krishna told his father to take him to the home of Yashoda and Nanda, who were close family friends. Yashoda had just given birth to a baby girl, and Nanda was to exchange baby Krishna with that baby girl.

The doors of the palace mysteriously opened while all slept. Vasudeva carried out Shri Krishna's instructions, soon returning to the dungeon with the baby girl. The palace awoke. A furious Kamsa—the malevolent king—came down to the dungeon, grabbed the baby girl, and prepared to throw her down on the stone floor as he had done with the six previous babies. But as he tried, she slipped out of his hands, flew up into the air, and appeared in her Divine form—the All Mother. She said to Kamsa, "You foolish king, I am the All Mother. You cannot kill me! The child you seek is elsewhere and will someday kill you."

Hiding in the Forest

For the next eleven years, Shri Krishna lived secretly in Vrindavan, unbeknownst to his cruel uncle Kamsa. In Vrindavan, Krishna was the beloved child or friend of everyone in his community. One might assume that if the Supreme Being came to Earth, it would naturally be with an obvious and constant display of his infinite power. However, Shri Krishna was playing, and teaching, a different game.

In this first stage of avataring, Shri Krishna lived in the country, out in the woods, with a simple, or apparently simple, cow-herding community. Shri Krishna's reasoning for this is straightforward: to keep power in the background and love in the foreground. This is the intimate and vital teaching for humans: in spite of being all-powerful, the Supreme Beings enjoy loving us infinitely more than displaying their power.

This paradox, and playfulness, is revealed in one of Krishna's many childhood stories.

Krishna Eating Dirt

Once when Krishna was three and his brother Balarama was four, the two were playing in the backyard. Suddenly Balarama called out to his mother, saying that Krishna was eating dirt again. Yashoda asked Krishna if this were true, to which Krishna replied that his brother was lying. He then opened his mouth and invited his mother to look in to see if he had eaten dirt. Looking in his mouth, Yashoda saw the entire Universe, endless planets, galaxies, the vastness of space, all beings, the Creator, everything. She paused for a moment and then said, "Oh well, it's time for your lunch."

God Almighty, as we call the Supreme Being in the West, had just shown his Earth mother the scope of all existence, but she voiced her preference: she would rather fix him lunch than see his almighty power. Again, this is one of the great secrets of the Ultimate Avatar. If we really understand, we will see that the sweetness of offering loving and intimate service is more fulfilling and enjoyable than beholding the Divine Absolute's power. Krishna's mother was really saying, "That's very nice that you have all this power, darling, but let's just keep playing as mother and son—it's so much more pleasurable."

During the eleven years of Krishna's childhood, all the residents of Vrindavan enjoyed some kind of sweet and intimate loving service with young Krishna. And they all greatly preferred this mood above seeing him as "God All Mighty." They knew who he was, but they believed that playing with him was far better than praying to him. Of course, Shri Krishna agrees.

Ordinarily, we are accustomed to thinking of ourselves as the children of a loving Father God, or Father and Mother God. Seen in terms of power, this makes perfect sense. But in Vrindavan, God/Bhagavan invented a game that is even more fun. As mind- or heart-bending as it sounds, He plays the baby, and we play the parents. For both Shri Krishna and us, this is much more fun, rewarding, and pleasurable. The games that the Avatar plays just for pleasure are called *lila* or "Divine play." This lila attitude of play is unique to the Vedic teachings and is a great secret to our relationship with the Supreme and Divine beings. And this play, this joy, calls to us—is a reminder to us—of our highest, eternal, blissful nature.

Eternal Games in Vrindavan

An even deeper secret is the story of youthful Shri Krishna's girl-friends, the *gopis*, and the love of his life, the spirit of his heart, on whom he has an eternal crush, the sweet and endlessly enchanting

Radha. She is actually Lakshmi, the eternal consort and Feminine Divine, the counterpart of Bhagavan, who lives eternally with him in the Transcendental realm of Vaikuntha. To see this subtle vision, try to be young and innocent again. Try to remember the sweet and magical, the first precious, innocent love of teenagers, the first truly sweet kiss, the first dance, holding hands and trembling with mystery and bliss. Now imagine that you, the atma, could play this game. Indeed—and I say this with immense joy and understanding—it takes great courage and playfulness for a man to become the sweet young boy in the bloom of youth. Bhagavan, as a young Krishna in the gopi-lila, plays your first but eternal love. This bliss—indeed, this memory—is the source of our sweetest love with whomever we love today.

Before we go any further into this sacred love story, let me say something on your behalf. The easiest way for you to hear these stories is with your adult brain, but then you will dismiss them as myths or fairy tales. Here in the material world, where power rules, you could easily doubt love, especially in the context of the All Powerful Being coming all the way to Earth and into our hearts to play love games with human beings.

Krishna knew that our world mind would naturally harbor these doubts. And so, throughout his eleven-year childhood in Vrindavan, a succession of very ugly and dangerous monsters would enter the peaceful countryside (in the spirit of these doubts). These endarkened souls, personified evil, would sneak into the idyllic Vrindavan and try to kill Krishna and his friends while they played. But every time they appeared, Krishna and his brother Balarama would effortlessly dispatch the evil demon with the push of a baby finger or the flip of a wrist.

To his friends, Bhagavan is all about love and play, but to those who want to go toe-to-toe with the Supreme Being and spoil his fun—in fact, to those who want to be Bhagavan—a flick of his Divine wrist is enough to send those thoughts personified onto their next birth.

Rasa Lila

Assuming I have for the moment dispelled your doubts that pure love is possible—and this is our ongoing struggle in life—let's return to young Krishna and his girlfriends, the gopis.

This relationship to the gopis is really a discussion about the possibility of love. In this world, we hear that "love makes the world go round." But equally, as we see with, say, Shakespeare's Romeo and Juliet, our love here is often sweet and then sad or even tragic. Our doubt is that lasting love is still possible to maintain in the Transcendental realm. The Ultimate Avatar's answer to our leaning toward no is a resounding, unstoppable YES! And not only that, but there is a full moon and a dance tonight—and every night—and you are invited.

In this book, I can share only a taste of this intoxicating wine. Shri Krishna is by definition more beautiful and more attractive than anyone, and the young gopis in the story represent the eternal souls who are madly in love with Krishna and want to be his lovers. He also loves them, but his beloved consort Radha is his eternal favorite.

One sweet evening, as the full moon began to rise over the blossoming and fragrant forest of Vrindavan, the beautiful Supreme Being, Shri Krishna, in the form of a sweet young boy, went into the deep forest and began to play his enchanting and magical melodies on his flute. Hearing this music, Radha and the gopis realized that the dance was about to begin. Mad with joy at the thought of Krishna, they dressed quickly, careless in their haste, and ran to the spot where young Krishna stood. If you received a personal invitation to a dance from the Supreme Lover of All, what would you do but hurry? So all the gopis and Radha ran to the clearing. Suddenly there were a hundred gopis, each with her own Krishna, who was holding her hands and looking into her eyes. The fortunate atmas, who had prayed for lifetimes for this moment, now held the Ultimate Avatar in their arms and danced the night away—into eternity.

When Krishna was eleven years old, his uncle Akrura drove a chariot to Vrindavan to take Krishna back to Mathura, the place of Krishna's birth. By this time, Krishna's uncle Kamsa knew where Krishna was and, as a ruse, invited Krishna to compete in an upcoming wrestling tournament, with the wicked intention of killing him.

As Akrura left with Krishna, Radha and the gopis stood in the path of the chariot with tears in their eyes. In the company of the gopis, Krishna had already revealed the deepest secrets of the atmas' eternal love with the Supreme Being. So one of the purposes of his descent had been accomplished. Neither he, nor Radha, his eternal counterpart, nor the gopis who had been advanced yogis for lifetimes would ever forget the mystery and magic of their full-moon dances together. Bathed in tears of ecstatic love, they said good-bye, for the moment, to the eternal Bhagavan, who now was always visible in the starlit sky of their hearts.

Krishna Restores Dharma

When Krishna and his older brother Balarama arrived in Mathura, they were greeted by a warrior elephant and two huge wrestlers who were under orders to kill Krishna. Instead, the hunted became the hunters, and after Krishna and his brother disposed of their attackers, Krishna personally killed his evil uncle Kamsa. The prophecy was fulfilled. Krishna then released Kamsa's father from prison and restored him as the righteous king of Mathura. Kamsa had been so confused and distorted that he had put his own noble father in the dungeon in order to usurp the throne.

For the next few years, Krishna and his brother, now reunited with their parents, Vasudeva and Devaki, proceeded with their royal education. No longer princes in exile, they resumed their royal station and were trained in all the arts and skills required of their noble birth. They were destined to be leaders.

In the nearby city of Hastinapura (north of what is now New Delhi), another drama was beginning to unfold, and this one would divide a nation, sweep everyone into an unavoidable, embittered entanglement, and set the stage for the fulfillment of the mission of the Ultimate Avatar on Earth as Bhagavan Shri Krishna.

Before descending from the Transcendental realm, Krishna instructed millions of beings to take birth in royal families throughout India. Among all of these beings were the very highest Devas and the most evil Asuras. It is crucial to understand that both of these irreconcilable opposites had taken birth in the most wealthy, noble, and influential royal families of that time. The most divine, including Krishna, and the most evil were now cousins.

All the players, some conscious, others still unconscious, were assembled, and the drama was ready to unfold. In the earlier epic, *Ramayana*, the forces of evil attacked from outside of Ram's royal family. He fought them and won, and restored the peace. But the *Mahabharata* takes place as the door to the age of quarrel is about to open, and in this thick, psychologically complex epic, the Devas and the Asuras were born into the same family—and both forces were related to the Ultimate Avatar.

An Epic Family Feud

The dharmic (good or more enlightened) brothers were called the *Pandavas*, while their evil, ignorant, or endarkened cousins were called the *Kauravas*. There were five Devic brothers in the Pandavas family, which was headed by the oldest brother, Yudhisthir, and his famous brother, Arjuna. On the Kauravas side of the family, there were one hundred evil brothers and one sister, all headed by the malicious Duryodhana. These two branches of the family were supposed to divide their vast family holdings evenly, but from a young age, Duryodhana was determined to kill his cousins and usurp their share of the property. Even as children, the Pandavas constantly faced deadly plots and schemes by their cousin and nemesis Duryodhana.

In this small book, we cannot begin to follow the twists of plot and the subtle nuances of the *Mahabharata*. It is a drama of epic proportions, a compendium of diplomacy and royal arts, a martial thriller, a mystery, a wide-ranging history covering thousands of years, a manual on leadership and strategy, an unparalleled cosmic chess match with multiple and simultaneous levels of meaning, an encyclopedia of the ancient world, a treasure trove of yogic wisdom, a secret window into the great mind of the Ultimate Avatar, an epic love story, and a saga of a war in which, it is said, over four million soldiers died in eighteen days—with no harm to the civilian population.

At the center of this epic story, ever present but slightly in the background, is the Avatar Shri Krishna. He is, of course, concerned about the outcome but honors the free will of all the players. Written and produced by the Avatar of political Krishna, himself the ultimate player, this cautionary tale remains to this day, and undoubtedly will for aeons, for our benefit. It is staged at the beginning of the age of Kali as a way to help us understand why dharma appears to be in exile and selfishness itself is so often dressed in royal robes.

The Dice Are Loaded

Once the Pandavas and Kauravas were adults, Duryodhana (of the Kauravas) hatched his final nefarious plan. It began with an apparently playful gambling match between him and his Pandava cousins. The dice, unsurprisingly to us, had been wickedly loaded in Duryodhana's favor. The betting became more and more intense until the Pandavas had lost all of their family wealth. Then they gambled themselves and then gambled the final prize: their wife, the beautiful Draupadi.

At the time, brothers were occasionally allowed to marry the same woman. For the sake of unity, the five Pandava brothers had married Draupadi, the most beautiful and wisest woman in India. She was also the representative of All Mother in human form. In the gambling match, the Pandavas lost her and finally were bound to thirteen years in exile, victims of Duryodhana's crooked games. To add insult to injury, Duryodhana commanded his brother to strip Draupadi naked in the open assembly, where thousands of men had gathered to watch the gambling.

Draupadi was dragged into the assembly by her hair. Her sari was pulled with the intention to leave her naked and to reveal her beauty to all the complicit onlookers. Her husbands were under guard and could do nothing. Draupadi held tightly to her sari with both hands. Then, she raised one hand, imploring Shri Krishna to save her. Finally, in desperation, she raised both arms and called out to Krishna. At that moment of surrender, Shri Krishna, the Supreme Being, incarnated as unlimited yards of sari material and no matter how long the wicked Dushasana, the brother of Duryodhana, pulled, he was unable to disrobe and humiliate Draupadi in front of the assembly.

After Queen Draupadi was saved from the clutches of Duryodhana's ignorance, she and the Pandavas were sent into thirteen years of exile, with the deal being that at the end of the exile, the Pandavas would finally receive their full right to half the kingdom. Their acceptance of exile rather than going to war with the cousins is one of the mysteries of the *Mahabharata*, and here much wisdom from the Avatar is revealed. The point is, by definition Devic beings always seek the good of all and never want war, even though Asuras, as endarkened beings, actually enjoy violence and cruelty and even instigate war due to their own selfishness and greed. So in the hope that war could be avoided, and for the good of all, the Pandava brothers and Draupadi accepted their long exile. Another meaning for the Pandava exile is that all dharmic or truthful people feel exiled when unscrupulous governments are in power.

Insatiable Greed

While Shri Krishna's dear cousins were in such a terrible dilemma, He was waiting for the opportune moment to strike back while simultaneously protecting them from a distance. When the time of the exile finally ended, the Pandavas came to Duryodhana to ask for their rightful share. His reply was an intractable no. War looked to be inevitable. Finally, in one last attempt, the Pandavas proposed that Duryodhana give them five villages, so they at least would have someplace to live. Their greedy cousin's reply is famous: "Not only will I not give you five villages, I would not give you enough land to drive the head of a needle." There was no longer any choice. War was the only answer.

A famous field was chosen for the conflict, large enough to hold millions of soldiers, horses, elephants, chariots, and military weapons. Its name was Kurukshetra. All the kings of India and beyond, in accordance with their warrior obligations and alliances, began to arrive at the battlefield to set up camp either on the side of the Pandavas or on the side of the Kauravas.

With the pressures and the complexities of life being what they are, as we all know, humans end up in so many unpredictable places, jobs, missions, and even wars that are neither of their making nor aligned with their true beliefs. Thus, not only were the two armies cousins from the same family, but their many relatives were there, distressingly, to fight against one another.

Several days before the war, Krishna arrived with seven divisions of soldiers. He called a meeting with Duryodhana and revealed himself to be the Supreme Being. He recommended a peaceful solution, but even then, Duryodhana refused to listen.

With the first day of battle soon approaching, Krishna instructed his friend and cousin Arjuna and his not-so-friendly cousin Duryodhana to meet with Him. Krishna explained that he would not be personally fighting in the war since his unlimited power would be an unfair advantage to the side he fought on. Instead, he explained, one of the two would get his armies and the other could have him as their adviser. Upon saying so, Krishna added, "I am going to my tent to take a nap. The first one I see upon waking will get first choice: me or my army." Retiring to his tent, the Supreme Lord put one chair at the head of his bed and one at the foot. Duryodhana arrived first. Proudly thinking of himself as the greatest ruler, Duryodhana sat in the chair by Krishna's head. Arjuna then arrived and sat at Bhagavan's feet. When Krishna awoke, he saw Arjuna first and said, "You have first choice."

Arjuna said, "My Lord, I will choose you as my adviser."

Krishna said, "Then I will be your chariot driver."

To this, Duryodhana exclaimed, "Excellent, I wanted your army from the beginning."

Ignorance Is the Enemy

Political Krishna had done his work; now it was time for the philosophical Krishna. Avatars descend with the purpose of revealing philosophical tools of divine wisdom to forgetful humans. The most compassionate take on this is to consider all the souls here—

including us—as sleeping and dreaming in varying degrees of forget-fulness of their real nature. The Vedas show us that there is only one enemy, and that is ignorance.

And so the *Mahabharata* is obviously in some ways a compendium and history of the times that preceded Krishna's appearance five thousand years ago. It is also a cautionary tale about the consequences of quarrels inside the family of mankind. Recognizing that all wars are between "cousins" and are painful for any sane person, we should view the epic as equally and urgently a story of the need for action when it comes to protecting Mother Earth and the innocent animals and humans that live upon Her body. The saying is: "Bad things happen when good people do nothing." The paradox presented in the *Mahabharata* is first about the wonderful and terrible consequences of human free will. At our best we are simply divine; at our worst we truly are . . . the worst.

Because this world is a campus, a place of learning, it goes without saying that we learn first by making mistakes. This means that life on Earth is messy and complicated, especially when many students forget why they are here. In the *Mahabharata*, the first strategy of the good cousins was to defer to evil in the hope of avoiding conflict. While this is a good immediate strategy, without eventual opposition the most selfish and ignorant students usually will rule the campus. If you follow the logic of sva-dharma, every-one is trying to work according to his and her bodily nature, and only one of the four work groups (thinker, protector, producer, laborer) will be charged with the duty of using force to protect the innocent.

The *Mahabharata* was important as an example because even the worst people on the field of battle knew better than to harm civilians with their fighting. This is an important lesson for our modern world. If we can inspire men of power not to harm the innocent, that will be a great lesson learned from the Avatar teachings. The next lesson for all people, according to their work natures, is to find the courage to resist and oppose evil with their powers. For producers, this means not making bad things; for thinkers, it is speaking eloquently against evil; for workers, it is refusing to labor for evil. For Arjuna in the *Mahabharata*, as wealthy ruler, his challenge was a huge armed conflict that could not be avoided. So as we approach his moment of conflict in the story, try to imagine that you are a billionaire, born into a military family and now find yourself a general and political leader with millions of lives resting on your protection. The two armies were lined up across from each other on the Kurukshetra field, beating drums and blaring trumpets and conch shells. The unthinkable was about to begin. Arjuna, the general on the side of good, was in a great chariot pulled by four white horses. Below him and holding the reins was Krishna, the Supreme Being and Ultimate Avatar, in the lowly job of chariot driver.

The Highest Truths Revealed

We are now ready to hear from philosophical Krishna delivering the concise messages of the Avatar in seven hundred verses of succinct teaching and instruction. You might think that a philosopher would be speaking in a café or town square. Instead we are about to hear the Avatar's summary of the PhD program while poised on the brink of an epic battle. The *Bhagavad Gita* begins with Arjuna saying, "O Krishna, please pull my chariot out into the middle of the field so I can see who has come to fight in this dreadful conflict." This was entirely unexpected! Arjuna knew everyone on the field, most on a first-name basis. Something was very wrong. Krishna pulled the chariot to the middle of the field and Arjuna began to speak.

Right there, freeze the action.

In chapter 10 we discussed Yoga, and how the Vedas describe a person in a human body as "riding in a chariot." The senses are horses, the mind is the reins, discernment is the driver, and the atma is the passenger. Here the metaphor is purposely repeated with one difference: instead of discernment being the chariot driver, or in this case, Arjuna's discernment being the chariot driver, Arjuna has the Supreme Being, his best friend and cousin, the Ultimate Avatar, as his chariot driver. If we are listening carefully, this is supposed to bring us to full attention. Is it possible that the Divine genius of the Supreme Being has designed the entire *Mahabharata* as a living instruction manual on the highest truths of Yoga seen in the context of human conflict? Could we, like Arjuna, invite the Supreme Being to replace our own limited discernment and become our driver as we face the day-to-day conflicts of the human race? If so, could it be that Arjuna is about to voice our doubts and fears and hear the wise responses of the Ultimate Avatar? Is this story a myth or a performance of eternal truth staged by the Supreme Being and His friends for our benefit five thousand years ago? We will have to decide.

Arjuna put down his bow and arrows, sat down on the chariot, and declared his unwillingness to fight. Trembling and with tears in his eyes, he told Krishna that he would rather go live in a cave or be killed unarmed and unresisting than fight against his own family. He told Krishna, "Now you are my guru, please tell me what to do." He then put his head in his hands and said, "I refuse to fight."

We do not have space here to recount the profound conversation that took place between a brilliant and compassionate human being and Bhagavan—the Person who is the very Source of everything. Their exact words are still recorded in the precise Sanskrit language, just as they were spoken five thousand years ago. Ever since then, this conversation has acted as the user's manual for the human condition and as the philosophical summary of Yoga and the entire Vedic Library. All the most important messages of the Avatar are coded in its clear verses. For millions, both in India and now outside, the *Bhagavad Gita* has been a daily guide to living in this world as an eternal being. It explains how to live with grace in this world and instructs on how to link with the Transcendental realm while living within matter. It is a beacon shining a light on the path to moksha—final freedom.

I Reside in Every Heart

A well-known passage summarizes Krishna's message to Arjuna. Bhagavan said: "I am the Source of everything; from Me the entire creation flows. Knowing this, the wise adore Me with all their hearts. Their thoughts dwell in Me, their minds are surrendered to Me, and they derive great satisfaction and bliss enlightening one another and conversing about Me. To those who are constantly devoted and remember Me with love, I give the understanding by which they may come to Me. Out of compassion for them, I, who am dwelling within their hearts, destroy, with the shining lamp of divine wisdom, the darkness born of ignorance.

By the end of the *Bhagavad Gita*, Arjuna is ready to act upon Krishna's message. He was restored to his greatest possible strength, remembering himself and others as eternal beings. Arjuna was then ready to face the ongoing daily challenge and joy of being alive in the material world.

At the end of the book, Shri Krishna said to Arjuna, "Have you heard Me with full attention, and is your misunderstanding now dispelled? If so, then you decide what you wish to do." Even after giving all His best advice, the Ultimate Avatar said, "Arjuna, you and all these atmas are eternally able to choose your truth, so now do whatever you want." And finally: "Please do not ever force or coerce anyone with this knowledge. Only teach My messages to wise, good-hearted souls who want to hear them."

In the end, my friends, it is our decision to drive our vehicles alone or to invite the Avatar to guide us, inform us, and inspire us.

FOURTEEN

THE SECRET OF SECRETS

Namaste, I see you becoming your greatest self, in a vow inspired by the Truth's descent. I see you healed and healing others, with unlimited bliss and endless love. I see your joyful eyes looking into the Avatar's, silently understanding the journey that all will make.

Although the Vedic Library has an immense wealth of knowledge we might assume everyone should hear, I hope the teachings of the Avatars make it absolutely clear that any form of coercion or pressured conversion is not considered appropriate behavior. Similarly, if you go to a regular library, you don't expect to be forced at gunpoint to read certain books. The point is to hear this knowledge on your own terms. To borrow a computer metaphor, the best way to download the Vedic "software" is in "demo mode," with no strings attached and no limited trial period. To further the metaphor, the best way to see the Vedas is as "software" while considering your mind and body as "hardware." Meditation, as it arose from Yoga, is the process of "running" profound ideas through the "hardware"—your mind and body—to see what capabilities and experiences are inspired. It is essential to remember that you are the student, so you are in charge. At the moment of death, you will fly your own airplane.

Knowing your friendly librarians (gurus) can certainly be useful, but they are only there to serve your learning. In this spirit, and with your permission, I will try in this final chapter to take you even deeper into the Avatar teachings—in demo mode, of course.

The Vedas say unequivocally that a human being can never collect enough material evidence to get to the absolute final conclusion. However, learning from the Avatar, we can download ideas that might otherwise be impossible to find by sifting through the fossils and bones of history alone.

Consider this question: Is the Universe custom or random? Let's begin pragmatically. Do you live in a custom-built or random-built house? The answer is self-evident: All homes are custom built.

How about computers: custom built or random built? Now, before you feel Big God barking into the equation or spot another creation/evolution argument on the horizon, please stop! Don't connect this to any dogma. I'm using these practical ideas to create an experience—your experience. In the journey of self-discovery, it is important to separate great ideas from the dogmas of religions or any other groups. One engineering definition of a computer is "purposeful intelligence in a box." Expanding the scale of that statement, what then is Mother Nature? Using the same definition, it is Purposeful Intelligence in a box, a vast biocomputer.

Here is where this is leading us: Yoga is the activity of connecting yourself to the Intelligence that pervades the cosmos. This is not sectarian. Anything that links you to the Intelligence of the Universe is "a Yoga." And anything that links you to the Intelligence of the Universe is a great thing.

In the end, you can see yourself in only one of two ways: either as a little intelligence surrounded by a random and unintelligent Universe or as a small intelligence surrounded by a great and caring Intelligence. In this equation, it is either yes to intelligence, or no. In this mode of thinking, let us ask: is the Universe supported by love or is it empty and uncaring?

The inimitable Albert Einstein asked the same thing: "The most fundamental question we can ever ask ourselves is whether or not the universe we live in is friendly or hostile." And he further commented that our answer to that question would literally *determine our destiny*. Insightful thinker, that Mr. Einstein.

The best way to try to answer these binary questions about "love or no love" is to ask, on a day-to-day basis, which would you prefer? I know which I prefer. If the Universe is empty and uncaring, what is the likelihood that love will flourish in the world around us or for us? Custom or random built? Intelligent or not? Supporting love or not? Friendly or hostile? And what is our greatest fear? On a bad day, is it not that we are alone in an endless, uncaring reality and that nothing really matters, existence is random and futile, and there is no love and no purpose?

The Avatars tell us that Ravana and Duryodhana—the despots of the two Indian epics—began their problematic journeys by first concluding that life is futile. The Avatars tell us that this is endarkened logic.

What then might remove such a doubt? Obviously, an awe-inspiring divine person descending to heal, love, and teach us and to protect life, truth, innocence, and dignity would go a long way to improving our mood.

One more question—and this is what the Avatars try to answer for us: If the Universe is indeed intelligent, loving, and purposeful, could the Being behind that existence make a gentle appearance here, a soft entrance? If this amazing cosmos is the result of divine loving Intelligence, could those same inconceivable Beings be as tender in love as They appear to be awesome in power?

Imagine that the Universe around us is actually an incredible science museum filled with precise, detailed and clear, exhibits and stunning inventions—say, planets that stay in orbit over millions of years, and Suns that burn constantly with a technology we can neither understand nor replicate. Indeed, why talk about space? Our own eye-to-brain connection is such a powerful computer that it makes more calculations in focusing for three seconds than can be done by the most powerful computer on Earth. What are we truly to think about all this?

If you did go to a mind-blowing, awe-inspiring museum and at the end of the tour someone said he or she knew the artist, who was having a party and invited you, would you go? So, is the descent of the Avatar a myth or a historical event? Is it possible, or is it not possible, that the Universe cares, that Someone loves? Does what we do matter or not? Though we are rarely conscious of it, every day we have this conversation with ourselves. This is the same conversation Arjuna had with Krishna. This is the same conversation Hanuman had with himself while getting ready to attempt the leap from India to Lanka while clutching Shri Ram's ring.

The story of the Avatar is the answer to the random or custom question. The Avatar's answer is clear: it's all custom.

There is a delightful tradition practiced in India that came from the Avatar culture. It relates to why visiting guests should be treated with much love and respect and generosity. The Sanskrit saying is *Atithi devo bhava*, which means, "The guest visiting may be a divine being." The Vedic culture understands that the Supreme Being must wear a disguise of some kind in order to appear within matter—and since an Avatar of one kind or another could come at any time, an unknown dinner guest may just be the Avatar. So the teaching informs us that it is best to treat all guests as Avatars coming to dinner. This is "Namaste, I see you" raised a level. The result is twofold: guests are inspired to be their highest divine selves; the host, in turn, by serving the guests as divine beings worthy of love, is doing an actual yogic practice, serving the Avatar.

When the Avatar came to Earth as Ram and Sita, or Krishna and all His friends and loves, the story tells us They were served and loved by everyone. Witnessing the embodiment of multiple flavors of love and service, we are given an example to follow. The Avatars' descent in our midst gives us role models for becoming our best divine selves.

Free to Love

According to the teaching, if you experience the story of the Avatar as a myth, the story remains in demo mode. There is also a process of installing the story of the Avatar within your heart so that it becomes properly and fully activated. When that happens, the story plays like a video—a "Ved-eo"—and your seeing the visions and feeling the emotions, drama, and love raise the possibility that our beautiful human story, our sweet and fragile eternal personhood, is actually real and has a blissful ending. When we are twice born, the first step of initiation reminds us that we are eternal beings full of as yet unrealized potentials. The second step has the Avatars revealing themselves inside us to show the way back to the Transcendental realm and to inspire us to new levels of committed action on behalf of dharma here.

For an unawakened atma, the Eternal Truth could avatar and not be seen, because the unawakened atma has not yet agreed to see the Avatar. Love does not and cannot use coercion or force. Love is inspired voluntary service, given with heartfelt enthusiasm. In the end, love is a decision—our decision.

In the film *Avatar*, the Indigenous Na'vi beings use their braided ponytails for forming a connection with nature and other beings. That image was taken directly from Vedic symbolism. In Sanskrit, that braid of hair is called the *sikha*. When a child is born, that part of the skull—the fontanel—is still soft and not yet closed. For yogis, that is the point of entry by which the atma comes into and leaves the physical body. In ancient times, and sometimes even today in India, children have that braid of hair while they are young students and are told that the Avatar will someday grab them by the sikha and lovingly pull them across to the Transcendental realm.

This book also includes a little pull—a call to remember, to notice, whether or not you are plugged in to the messages and voices of the Avatar and all the Devas and important realities around you. But downloading and hearing the voice of the Supreme Intelligence can't happen unless the link is made. Yoga is the science of making the link to the Transcendental Source of your true self.

After making the link, the next step is to form the bond. The Avatar descends into our midst as a beautiful and noble Supreme Person, so we can form the bond. The bond is possible only when we go out of the demo mode and see the Avatar as eternally real and capable of deep love—more real than the inert matter that surrounds us. The bond is formed when all our devotion and love is gathered together from all the things and beings we love and is refocused with one-pointedness on the image and person of the Avatar. The re-forming of this bond is the reason why Shri Ram and Sita Devi and Bhagavan Shri Krishna and His many friends came to Earth to reattract us in the first place. They are here to encourage us to reestablish our lost or wavering belief that Love, Beauty, Light, and Truth are eternal and always endure.

You might at first think that focusing all our love, thought, and devotion on the Persons of the Avatar could cause us to withdraw from life and our relationships with others. The effect instead is the realization that the Avatar holds a vision of that same love with all atmas—no matter how those souls appear to us at any moment. This means that Shri Ram loved Ravana just as much as He loved Sita Devi. It was only Ravana who had temporarily forgotten how to love. Ram's wish for Ravana was not that he die or be punished, but that he be restored to his true beautiful, loving, and eternal nature. When Krishna "killed" an asura, it was to remove the gu covering the atma—causing that atma to forget its true nature. The Vedas say it this way: With marriage, partners become connected to all the relatives on both sides. The bond of marriage binds us to all the beings our partner loves. So what if, like Hanuman, you deeply served Shri Ram, or if, like Arjuna, you were Shri Krishna's very best friend, and you came to find out that your Divine master or friend actually loves everyone? Not just some beings, not just the pretty ones or the famous ones, but everyone—the good, the bad, and the ugly.

Some might have thought that the problem with the University metaphor is that the more advanced students would look down upon the students in lower grades, abusing them, calling them ignorant, and judging them harshly from their own lofty tower of learning. It does happen. This is precisely the reason why we need higher role models of great integrity to guide us in how to avoid such pitfalls. The Avatar's love and concern for every living being shows us by example that some do have higher knowledge, but greater love, devotion, and humility is vital to keep it in balance. In the *Ramayana*, a bridge is built to Lanka thanks largely to the mighty Hanuman's throwing huge boulders out to sea, one after another. Between his legs, a small squirrel is tossing grains of sand toward the sea. In a booming voice, Hanuman says, "Ho there, little squirrel, be careful, we are doing important work here for Shri Ram." Ram looks over at Hanuman and says, "Ho, Hanuman, that squirrel is doing just as much as you."

A Vow of Love

Within the word *Avatar* is another secret Sanskrit word that guides us to the next level of our development. The word is *vrata*, made from the same letters as Avatar. *Vrata* means "a vow or commitment"—a giving of our word that then governs and directs our behavior. This is the healing medicine for the irresponsible use of free will by humans. Animals are what they are by nature and instinct, but humans advance or degrade ourselves according to the greater vision that we bind ourselves to through a conscious and purposeful vow.

It is often said that "it isn't what you know, it's whom you know." The Vedas say both are crucial. Our knowing of the ritam, the Laws of Nature, allows us to cooperate with Mother Nature and create a more harmonious life and world. Learning to know the Devas, the divine helpers in the Material Nature, gives us excellent role models of divine service, which leads us toward deeper compassion and enlightenment. However, there remains within us a potential that can be activated only by an association with someone who inspires us to be the most noble person we are capable of being. If, as the film *Avatar* points out, at our worst we are mining the world for *Unobtanium*, then the Avatar comes bearing the medicine of Divine inspiration, the "Restorium."

Once we form the link to the Transcendental and the bond with the Person of the Avatar, then we take a vrata that our lives will be dedicated to living up to the noble ideals expressed in the lives of the Avatars. That vow becomes the new guiding principle in our lives. Imagine a world filled with souls who live in the service of all beings, inspired by the loving example of the Avatar.

That final stage of initiation and inspiration is not accomplished by joining a group. It is not limited by geography, nationality, age, race, politics, religion, or any other material consideration. Once the eternal individual has chosen to follow the inspiration of the Avatar, then the realization comes that the Divine Intelligence is in control of the final outcome of all situations and activities. Living in that state of mind is called surrender—not surrender because of domination, but surrender as trust. This is the meaning of Arjuna's having

Shri Krishna drive his chariot across the field of Kurukshetra. Our bond with the Avatar is expressed as our desire for Divine Guidance and service. In the *Bhagavad Gita*, that state is called karma yoga, which means putting all that we have learned to the test by living in this world in the service of the Avatar and working for the good of all beings.

What we need are heroes and heroines. We need great souls, mahatmas, who only want the good of all, and who do everything with an ear to the lips of the Divine voice of the Avatar. Our Avatar moment is realized when we live with and for the good of all beings in mind and heart. The Avatar moment of our world will be realized if we can all serve one another and evolve together in divine cooperation. This is the hope of the Avatars and the secret of the messages They left during Their appearance among us.

As at the beginning of my sharing these Vedic visions, I need to bow humbly before my many teachers from all cultures with gratitude and respect. The guru, or guide, is merely a messenger trying to be of some small service to the Avatar. The tools and teachings in this book were given to me in sacred trust by my gurus and teachers from India. They were trying to serve the Avatars and so, in their love and courageous wisdom, have given their greatest treasure to the grandchildren of their colonizers. I bow to them in respect and gratitude and hope some of the sweet visions of the Avatars shine through the pages of this book and bless those who hear and see its messages. Any faults within it are my own. Namaste—I see you all and bow to the divine within you. Jai Sita Ram, Jai Shri Krishna, may all be fed, may all be safe, may all find peace, and may all be free.

Your messenger from the Avatars,
Kavindra Rishi

(ΩΕΔΙΤΑΤΙΟΝS ΑΝΔ

ΡΚΑCΤΙCΕS

Chapter 1

Take a moment to reread and meditate upon this chapter's Namaste greeting.

Practice 1: Commit to trying to live as the atma all day. Witness your body, mind, and thoughts as beautiful yet temporary and separate from your truest self. You are the consciousness that pervades your mind and body. Because you're eternal, be kind to yourself when you forget this.

Practice 2: Do the same as above, all day, but with everyone you meet. See each one more deeply, for who he or she truly is—as the atma. Choose a Namaste-like greeting that reminds you to do this every time you meet someone.

Practice 3: Spend the day imagining you are not from here and are only visiting. You are eternal—only temporarily enrolled in the University of Matter—and are originally from the Transcendental.

Chapter 2

Take a moment to reread and meditate upon this chapter's Namaste greeting.

Practice 1: Commit to one day of believing you are never alone, that you are surrounded by Divine Intelligence, and that the entire Universe, including your own body, is operating that way. Give thanks for this at several prearranged moments in the day. In this way, try to see all that surrounds you as the All Mother, the Divine Mother, in loving support of your life.

Practice 2: Walk in nature and meditate upon the processes of nature and the Laws of Nature as being run by great beings (Devas). Remember that this is the same for all the systems in your body. Though not your true self, your body is of great importance on the journey of life.

Practice 3: Since the Indigenous cultures are healthy because of their sustainable lifestyle, make a list of all the purchases, actions, or lifestyle choices you make, and ask yourself if they are sustainable or not. How could they be improved? Commit to cutting back on the unsustainable and increasing the sustainable.

Chapter 3

Take a moment to reread and meditate upon this chapter's Namaste greeting.

Practice 1: Commit to planting a tree once a year, somewhere, in the understanding that trees are the lungs of our species. Walk in nature and meditate upon the relationship between your breath and the trees' "breath," and how interrelated you both are, in every moment.

Practice 2: Make a list of a few of your IQ strengths and your WeQ strengths and meditate upon how each one can serve another on the journey to developing your 3rd IQ.

Practice 3: Commit to taking times in your workday to break for several minutes, observe your breath, and place your focus behind your eyes, which develops our 3rd IQ. Smile, remembering that you are an eternal, divine being.

Chapter 4

Take a moment to reread and meditate upon this chapter's Namaste greeting.

Practice 1: Take time during the day to close your eyes and relax for a moment until you feel the flow of energy in your fingertips (without touching your fingertips). This is an interior experience and an awareness of your prana—life force—flowing through its channels. Be aware that what you think, say, and hear shapes who you are and who you will become. Practice being conscious of speaking truth kindly to yourself and others.

Practice 2: Take short breaks in your workday to stretch your body— do yoga asanas (postures) if you know any—and do them with an awareness that you are trying to keep the prana (life force) flowing. Remember to do all of these moves in a balanced way, without excessive strain, and with your breath flowing smoothly.

Practice 3: Minimize all the unnecessary or uninspired sound vibrations in your life—gossip, mindless television, talk radio, unharmonious music. Take time alone to learn and practice a mantra. Chant aum, listening to the sound of the vibration, chanting out loud if you can, loosening any tightness in your throat, relaxing any tension.

Chapter 5

Take a moment to reread and meditate upon this chapter's Namaste greeting.

Practice 1: Wake up at sunrise to meditate upon the direct link between ourselves, our own biological mothers who gave rise to us, and Mother Earth, who gives rise to all of life here. Just as you would protect your own mother, ask how you can do the same for Mother Earth.

Practice 2: Take Practice 1 a step further and meditate upon the idea that all life arises from the inseparable interaction of male and female beings and energies. Consider how this mysterious process is sacred. Reflect upon how your relationships serve or undermine this larger reality.

Practice 3: Meditate upon the natural world around you, and observe which part is the male and which is the female, or Shakti. View the "essence" as female and the "structure that holds" that essence as male. Recall that the fragrance of the rose is its Shakti, and the flower that holds the fragrance is the male component.

Chapter 6

Take a moment to reread and meditate upon this chapter's Namaste greeting.

Practice 1: Review the definition of *karma*. Meditate on the simplicity of karma as nothing more than cause and effect, and remember that the effects are neither rewards nor punishments but are the universal Laws of Nature responding to all that we do, from the law of gravity to the moral consequences of our thoughts and actions.

Practice 2: Meditate upon the definition of *dharma* as the very essence of a thing. When using things, or working with people, try to see their essential natures rather than projecting your desires onto them. Remember that all things and all beings have a dharma, an essential nature. Meditate upon your own dharma—physical, mental, spiritual—and ask what knowing it would do to the way you live. Ask yourself how you could "live your dharma," supporting the most good and causing the least harm possible.

Practice 3: Be a leader at work. Ask yourself if your company's products and its push for profits also support the well-being of others and are environmentally sustainable. Ask yourself if there is anything else you can do to expand the way you and your colleagues replenish anything you disturb.

Chapter 7

Take a moment to reread and meditate upon this chapter's Namaste greeting.

Practice 1: Meditate upon the difference between your dreaming and waking states and how the Avatars tell us our waking state is also a dream we are trying to wake up from. Ask yourself where you would be if you woke up.

Practice 2: In the spirit of being twice born, meditate upon the person you would be if you were to let go of the "old stories" that keep you trapped in the past or worrying too much about the future. With your eyes closed, imagine that those stories are held in your body—feel them—and then smile-release them, knowing that you are not the body, or those stories.

Practice 3: Meditate upon Bhumi dharma and the ways Mother Earth has supported you through food, shelter, air, water, warmth, and all countless other blessings you receive. Ask yourself how you can repay this selfless giving of Mother Nature by restoring, sustaining, and protecting Her.

Chapter 8

Take a moment to reread and meditate upon this chapter's Namaste greeting.

Practice 1: No matter what challenges you have faced with family, show gratitude to your parents for the gift of your life! Meditate upon the idea that you and they are eternal beings who chose to have this human experience as an essential part of rediscovering your true natures.

Practice 2: With the metaphor of cell phones in your mind, meditate upon the possibility that the Universe and your own atma, your body, and Nature are constantly sending wireless signals to you for your well-being. Relax and be open to listening to these many channels of vital information.

Practice 3: Commit yourself to really speaking with kindness and respect to elders. Ask them what they have learned about life and which teachings have really made a difference to them. Remember to remember that they, too, are beautiful atmas and a valuable resource just waiting to be of service.

Chapter 9
Take a moment to reread and meditate upon this chapter's Namaste greeting.

Practice 1: Meditate upon the idea that the point of being here is to have a life full of deep experiences that move us toward ultimate freedom. At the same time, look for the path of least friction and harm in all you do. Consider that this positive tension of responsible freedom is a powerful self-refining process.

Practice 2: Meditate upon the remarkable truth that real freedom is by definition constrained or bound by Nature's laws. In other words, freedom comes through cooperation. Study what it means to be free. Observe carefully what constraints will give you the most freedom.

Practice 3: Meditate on the idea that all beings—not just humans— are actually atmas, and that we are all in school, trying to progress in the difficult and beautiful material world.

Chapter 10
Take a moment to reread and meditate upon this chapter's Namaste greeting.

Practice 1: Using the metaphor of the six blind men studying many parts of the elephant, meditate on how all truths in this world are only partial. Meditate on how you can resist the desire to force your views on others. Remember how obvious it is that you know much more than you did ten years ago. Assume you will know much more again in another ten years.

Practice 2: Review the definition of *Yoga*. Meditate upon the idea that Yoga is anything that links you to your true self (atma) and the Devic beings who support you on your journey. Discover the process—observing the breath, chanting, meditative walking—that most quickly links you to something greater than the limitations that keep us small.

Practice 3: Pretend you are a turtle, and practice withdrawing your senses from their objects and addictions. Fast for a day, change your pattern of consumption. Make your senses go without for periods of time until the horses no longer drag you here and there.

Chapter 11

Take a moment to reread and meditate upon this chapter's Namaste greeting.

Practice 1: Review again the definition and ideas of the Transcendental. Commit to taking time every day to meditate upon the Transcendental, or what that might feel like. When trying to link to your higher self—the atma—recall that the Avatars tell us that our awareness, our consciousness, is direct evidence of the atma. Meditate also on the idea that your atma illuminates your body "like the Sun illuminates the world."

Practice 2: Meditate upon all of your memories and any self-stories as a collection of wonderful but temporary mementos. In your meditations, or whenever these mementos arise, practice letting them go in the knowledge that they are not your true self. Do this with gratitude.

Practice 3: Meditate on your heart, and with even breath fill yourself with the emotion of a love bigger than anything you've ever experienced. Feel that you are made for eternal love. Feel the gratitude and the joy of that love radiating from within your heart. Feel that emotion connecting you (your shining atma) and the Transcendental Divine Person, Bhagavan.

Chapter 12

Take a moment to reread and meditate upon this chapter's Namaste greeting.

Practice 1: Meditate on the idea of the exile being the exile of ourselves from divine love and the Transcendental realm. Meditate on the idea of Sita's kidnapping as our own beautiful atma being pushed and pulled and bossed around in the material world by greedy and ravenous overlords.

Practice 2: Meditate on Hanuman's devotion to Ram as your own devotion and love, expressed as service for all beings, and for the Divine beings, and to the endless journey of learning to be your delicious, wonderful, shining self.

Practice 3: Allow yourself to experience really big emotions (love, gratitude, joy, sadness), but express them carefully, with sensitivity to the sensibilities of others. Ecstasy should always be tempered by humility. This prevents fanaticism.

Chapter 13

Take a moment to reread and meditate upon this chapter's Namaste greeting.

Practice 1: Reread chapter 13 to familiarize yourself with the story and the characters in the *Mahabharata*. Meditate on the possibility that the story is true. Observe how that feels. Meditate on the epic as a morality tale. Meditate on the psychology of the story as something going on inside both your mind and your body, an epic version of your own story.

Practice 2: Commit to finding a good translation of the *Bhagavad Gita* (the literal compendium of the Avatars teaching) and read it with time to contemplate its teachings.

Practice 3: A famous line in the *Bhagavad Gita* (deep in the *Mahabharata*) says: "Armed with Yoga, stand and fight." Meditate upon what this seemingly paradoxical statement is asking of you. In the process of that meditation, think of dharma, karma, your own atma, and standing up for whatever you believe to be for the good of all.

Chapter 14

Take a moment to reread and meditate upon this chapter's Namaste greeting.

Practice 1: Review the definition of *Yoga*. Meditate on what it means when we say that Yoga is a link. With whom or what do you long to link? These are the choices available to your true self: the empty Transcendental (Nirvana), the effulgent light of eternity (Brahman), and the eternal realms of beauty and love (Vaikuntha Loka). What causes the bond?

Practice 2: Review the definition of the Avatar and the definition of the Transcendental. Meditate on how a growing relationship with the Avatar and the Avatar's teaching creates a bond. Mediate on how this bond is necessary for the leap to the Transcendental. Remember, imagination is the first step to creating possibility.

Practice 3: Meditate on remembering that you are a divine, beautiful, wonderful, eternal being—an atma. You are in a temporary University in the material world. You are surrounded by Divine beings (friends, strangers, invisible Devas). You are surrounded and supported by the Divine Mother and an ultimate Supreme Being who wants nothing more than the sweetest intimacy with you. Please be gentle to yourself and remember the Ultimate Avatar.

wisdom of the Avatars

Chapter 1

1. All living entities are eternal Divine beings called atmas.

2. There is an ever-existing Transcendental world, as well as our temporary material world.

3. Avatars are descents of the Supreme Being come to our world to heal the Earth and teach us our true nature.

Chapter 2

1. Nature is a Being called the All Mother or Mother Nature.

2. Her angels or divine helpers are called Devas and conduct the Laws of Nature.

3. Working together with Mother Nature is the best path for the good of all.

Chapter 3

1. The word *truth* comes from the word *tree*, showing our deep relationship and interdependence with trees.

2. The body is built on branching structures just like a tree.

3. Understanding the Law of Entropy is the key to restoring the balance of life

Chapter 4

1. Prana, vitality, or the life force is the secret of healthy living and preventative medicine.

2. Combining the healing arts and food with emergency medicine is the new health ideal.

3. The use of sound vibration is the most powerful means of energetic healing.

Chapter 5

1. Female beauty is a reflection of the Feminine Divine.

2. Shakti, or the female energy of everything in nature, helps us understand the integrated view of male and female.

3. The return of Divine Feminine Wisdom is crucial for healing the planet.

Chapter 6

1. Dharma, or using everything according to its nature, is the basis of creating a healthy lifestyle.

2. The Indigenous worldview says no one can truly own the Earth's resources—they belong to the Great Mother, and the land is sacred.

3. The Avatar tells us there are four predominant work categories based on individual human propensity: thinkers, warriors, producers, and servers. They are all vital parts of the social body.

Chapter 7

1. It is extremely difficult but vital, on the spiritual journey, to remain aware of one's divine eternal nature.

2. Dreaming is a type of out-of-body experience where we park the gross body and experience the subtle body.

3. Excessive IQ thinking (lacking EQ) can thicken the mental ego shell, making it as impenetrable as the physical body.

Chapter 8

1. Wise elders need to be listened to if we are to learn how to sustain life.

2. Avatars descend to Earth to defend Mother Nature from destructive actions of cruel and selfish humans.

3. The Avatars implore us to stand up against social injustice, feel the pain of the unprotected and, by doing so, demand their protection.

Chapter 9

1. Atmas come to the material world to completely experience matter, which is considered the material aspect of the Supreme Being.

2. The Avatar says we should all be allowed to think, speak, and meditate any way we like, as long as we do not cause harm to others.

3. Understanding the food chain and holding sustainability and animals as sacred are essential. In this way, purchasing food becomes an empowering, political act for the good of all.

Chapter 10

1. Yoga is the technology by which you learn to link to whatever you focus on, ideally your true self and the Supreme Beings.

2. The Avatars tell us it is extremely important for spiritual growth that we each understand the best requirements for our particular physical body.

3. Ashtanga yoga explains what are called the eight limbs of Yoga.

Chapter 11

1. To be liberated, we not only have to let go of all the joys and sorrows of the past, but we also must give up our attachments to any future outcome within matter.

2. The Vedas tell us there are three possible Vedic spiritual conclusions: (1) Transcendental Nirvana (emptiness), (2) Akshara Brahman (oneness), and (3) Vaikuntha Loka (eternal transcendental individuality). We choose where we want to go.

3. The Ultimate Avatars descend from the Transcendental realm.

Chapter 12

1. The *Ramayana* is one of two great epics from India where the Supreme Being chooses to avatar for the good of the planet and humanity.

2. In the *Ramayana*, the Supreme Being has chosen to avatar as Ram, the great *raj* ("king"), with His wife Sita and all of Their friends.

3. The *Ramayana* is known as an exemplar of devotion in partnership and a manual on how to be a noble leader.

Chapter 13

1. The *Mahabharata* is the other Indian epic. It is also about Avatars descending to Earth in order to restore harmony and teach divine wisdom.

2. In the *Mahabharata*, the Supreme Being has chosen to avatar as Krishna, Radha, and all Their friends to demonstrate pure Divine Love.

3. At the end of the *Bhagavad Gita*, Krishna, although He is the Supreme Being, says He will not tell anyone what he or she must do. We all have to choose our own paths.

Chapter 14

1. One of the biggest decisions we have to make is whether we believe the Universe is custom or random, loving or void of love, friendly or hostile.

2. Humans progress spiritually by taking purposeful vows (vratas) and sticking to them.

3. Karma yoga is realizing we can control our actions but not the outcomes of our actions and then surrendering the outcomes to the Supreme Being.

GLOSSARY

Aboriginal: "With the origin" or aware of the "original intention" of life.

Adam and Eve: From the Sanskrit *Jiva Atma*. Eve is from the Hebrew *Heve* or "life." The *J* in Jiva and the *E* in Eve were eventually changed to *Vi*, giving us *vive*, and then to *L*, giving the word *live*.

Adi Shankara: [A-di-shan-car-a] Great teacher of Advaita Vedanta.

Advaita: [A-dvai-ta] Nondual, often referring to the Vedantic teachings of Shankaracarya and similar Vedantins who emphasized the undifferentiated Brahman state as the final goal of Yoga practice. His conclusion denies the ultimate reality of the material world and postulates that neither the soul nor the Supreme Being exists as distinctive individuals in the final state of homogenized Being.

Aham Brahmasmi: [Ah-ham Bra-mas-mi] "I am identical with, the same in nature as, the Brahman existence."

Ahamkara: [Ah-hum-ka-ra] Indicates the first and most subtle energy of matter, which, when combined with the consciousness of the atma, creates the idea that we come from and are the same as matter.

Akshara Brahman: [Ak-sha-ra Bra-man] *Akshara* means "imperishable," the supreme abode of immortality. *Brahman* means "the unlimited, unified, and ever-expanding field of Transcendental existence."

Anna: [Ah-na] Sanskrit, referring to food, the concept being that what you eat affects your energy and then your mind.

Anusvara: [Ah-nus-va-ra] A special Sanskrit letter that produces the "ung" sound in om.

Apsaras: [Ap-sa-ras] The sensual Divas of the Devas.

Archetype: An original model of a person, ideal example, or proto-type from which others are copied, patterned, or emulated.

Arjuna: [Are-ju-na] The third of the five Pandava brothers. A great bowman, he figured prominently in winning the Kurukshetra battle, with Krishna driving his chariot. It was to Arjuna that Krishna spoke the *Bhagavad Gita* just before the battle.

Asana: [Ah-sa-na] Restraining, checking, holding back, preventing, controlling; restriction, fixed role, necessity. Yogic postures for correctly channeling the life force, healing, and bringing the body to a state of stillness and balance for the purpose of yogic meditation.

Ashram: [Ash-ram] In India, a religious hermitage, typically located far from human habitation.

Astra: [As-tra] Mantra-powered weapons used by the Divine brothers in the *Ramayana*.

Astrology: See *Jyotish*

Asura: [Ah-su-ra] Literally means those who have chosen to oppose the light. In the cosmos, these beings cause chaos by opposing the order of the Devas. On Earth, humans can choose to become asuric.

Atithi devo bhava: [A-tea-thrr day-vo ba-va] The guest may be God/an Avatar.

Atma: [Ah-tma] The true self that cannot die and is eternally conscious and joyful by nature.

Atomic: Of a very small particle.

Avatar: [Ah-va-tar] Literally one who descends voluntarily; *Ava* to save others and *tara* to help them cross over matter to the Transcendental realm. Incarnation is a process forced upon a soul, whereas an Avatar is a voluntary descent of either the Supreme Being from the Transcendental or a Deva from the higher material realms into the human realm of matter.

Ayodhya: [A-yod-ya] Shri Ram's father's, Dasaratha's, capital city in the *Ramayana*.

Ayurveda: [Aye-yur-vay-da] *Ayus* means "life"; Ayurveda is the medical system based on Vedic wisdom. It creates well-being by supporting the life force in various ways.

Balarama: [Ba-la-ra-ma] Krishna's older brother in the *Mahabharata*.

Banyan trees: Vast primordial trees under which schools of yogic learning were held in India.

Bhagavad Gita: [Bha-ga-vad Ghee-ta] Sacred Hindu scripture of seven hundred verses contained within the *Mahabharata*, summarizing Vedic philosophy spoken by Shri Krishna.

Bhagavan: [Ba-ga-van] The Supreme Person who is the source of and possessor of all six qualities or opulences: wealth, fame, knowledge, beauty, renunciation, and strength.

Bharata: [Ba-ra-ta] The region we now call India; also the name of Ram's noble brother in the *Ramayana*.

Bhumi: [Boo-me] Mother Earth.

Brahman: [Bram-an] The Creator of the Universe.

Brahmin: [Bram-in] Those who know Brahman through the Vedic wisdom and who carry and reveal the flame of that truth to society. Also those who are intellectual by nature, by their sva-dharma or primary working ability.

Brahmajyoti: [Bra-ma-joe-ti] The Transcendental light of eternal, conscious, and joyful existence.

Dandaka: [Dan-da-ka] Deep forests in the *Ramayana*.

Darshan: [Dar-shan] From the root *dhristi*, which means "vision." The guru gives the student a darshan of spiritual principles and realizations. There are six darshans, or ways of seeing the truth, taught in the Vedas.

Dasaratha: [Da-sa-ra-tha] The king of Ayodhya, who is also Ram's father in the *Ramayana*.

Demi-god: A child born as the result of a union between a Deva and a human.

Devaki: [Day-va-key] Lord Krishna's birth mother and the wife of Vasudeva. Her brother was Kamsa, the evil king who wished to kill Krishna.

Devanagari: [Day-va-na-ga-ri] "The city of the Devas"; refers to the written Sanskrit script or the Sanskrit alphabet.

Devas: [Day-vas] Derived from the Sanskrit *div*, meaning "to play in the light." These beings are also called the divine helpers. They are atmas just like humans or animals, but they have attained posts in the administration of the laws of material Nature. In short, they work for Vishnu and Lakshmi in the job of maintaining Mother Nature.

Devis: [Day-vis] The feminine plural of Devas.

Dharana: [Da-ra-na] The limb of Patanjali's Ashtanga Yoga Sutras that deals with the nature and the control of the mind. It reaches the techniques of mental focus, one-pointedness, clarity, and inner vision. The mind is the king of the senses, and dharana is the crown of yogic knowledge, teaching how to remove unconscious habits, impressions, and tendencies. Just as a dam holds water without tension, the yogis say, so the mind should be one-pointed in dharana, to prepare for the next limb, dhyan, or meditation.

Dharma: [Dhar-ma] Another essential Sanskrit word, from the root *ri dhri*, translates as "the essential nature of a thing, which, if taken away, renders that thing no longer itself." From *dhri* comes the word *dharma*. Dharma has no equivalent word in English but can be translated as "using everything according to its divinely intended nature." Everything, including all of us as individual atmas, has an essential Divine nature, which determines the right use of the thing (the *ri* in *right* also comes from *ritam*). To use a thing in the *right* way is a ritual—*ri* again. And today, science is simply rituals that work with the true nature of a substance to consistently produce a predictable result. *Dhri* is the same as the root *tri* (as in *tree* and *truth*), as we discussed earlier. The *tr*, *dr*, and *rt* are all related at their root. We as atmas, all the way down to the smallest atom in existence, all have a specific dharma, or right way of being used or acting.

Dhri: [Dree] Sanskrit root, the essential nature of a thing, which, if taken away, renders that thing no longer itself.

Dhyan: [Dy-an] The central limb of the eight-limbed Ashtanga Yoga, which means "meditation." In China the word was pronounced *chan*; in Japan it became *zen*. There are many kinds of meditations prescribed in the Vedas, each leading the practitioner to specific goals, powers, and states of being.

Draupadi: [Dro-pa-dee] The Pandavas' beautiful wife in the *Mahabharata*; she was gambled away by Yudhisthir and almost forcibly disrobed in front of an assembly of men, a significant event dishonoring the feminine that signaled the impending start of the war.

Dukkha: [Du-ka] Buddha's conclusion that the world is a place of suffering caused by everyone's desire for and attachment to matter; understanding this leads to the liberation that comes from not owning any matter or having any material desires.

Duryodhana: [Dur-yo-da-na] The eldest son of Dhritarashtra and chief rival of the Pandavas. He made many attempts to cheat the Pandavas of their rightful share of the Kuru kingdom. After arrogantly ignoring the good advice of Bhishma, Drona, and Krishna, he perished with his ninety-nine brothers in the Kurukshetra battle.

Dvaita: [Dvai-ta] Literally "distinctive." When applied to Vedantic philosophy, the word refers to the distinctivist teachings of Madva, who taught that there is more than one category of real eternal existence and thereby emphasized the unique individuality of all beings and things. Dvaita recognizes the distinction between the Supreme Being and the individual jiva souls.

Dwija: [Dwee-ja] Second birth.

Eve: From the Hebrew *heve* or "life."

Gate gate paragate parasamgate bodhi svāhā: "Gone, gone, gone beyond, gone beyond beyond and given to pure knowing."

Gopis: [Go-peas] In the rural setting of Vrindavan, the young girls would milk the cows and turn the milk into various foods. During Bhagavan Shri Krishna's appearance as an Avatar, those girls were really yogis reincarnated from a previous life who had taken birth to have the experience of being the girlfriend or lover of Bhagavan Shri Krishna as a part of His revelation as purna, or complete, Avatar.

Gu: [Goo] Matter.

Guna: [Goo-na] The state, quality, condition, or mode of a material thing; there are three gunic states of matter: the creative, the maintaining, and the destructive.

Guru: [Goo-ru] Literally "heavy;" the implication that one who is filled with knowledge of the Supreme Eternal Truth becomes heavy. Also, "gu-remover."

Gurukulas: [Gu-ru-ku-las] Traditional residential schools in India usually run by husband and wife teams.

Hanuman: [Ha-nu-man] The monkey general who became the hero of the *Ramayana*; was the Avatar of the Deva Vayu.

Intelligence Quotient (IQ): A score derived from one of several different standardized tests designed to assess logical intelligence.

Ishvara: [Eesh-va-ra] "Lord or controller"; in nature, the Devas are all in control of various forces of nature. That control makes them Ishvara. Above all those lesser Ishas or Lords is the Parama Ishvara, or the Supreme Lord, Shri Krishna.

Ishvara Pranidhan: [Eesh-va-ra Pra-knee-dan] The process of learning to know and correctly respect the Ishas, either Devas or the many forms of the Supreme Being.

Janaka: [Ja-na-ka] A great king in the *Ramayana*, also Sita's father.

Jiva-atma: [Jee-va-ah-tma] Air-breathing atmas.

Jyotish: [Jo-teesh] The Sanskrit word for "astrology;" the science of how life is regulated by light over time, manifested in space.

Kaballah: Jewish mystical path.

Kaikeyi: [Kay-key-yi] Dasaratha's youngest and favorite wife in the *Ramayana*.

Kali Yuga: [Kul-lee] The fourth age, or Iron Age, in the Yuga cycle, which has a duration of 432,000 Earth years. As of 2010, we are 5,116 years into Kali Yuga.

Kalpa Vriksha trees: [Kal-pa Vreek-shah] Kalpa refers to a great length of time in Hindu/Vedic cosmology, specifically 4,300,000,000 years, or one day of Brahma. Kalpa Vriksha trees yield any kind of fruit that is desired and exist only in the Transcendental.

Kamsa: [Calm-sa] Evil king in the *Mahabharata* who was ultimately killed by Krishna.

Karma: [Car-ma] Another essential Sanskrit word from the root *ri*. From it we derive the root word *kri*, meaning "to do"; the law of cause and effect. The modern scientific idea that every action has an equal and opposite reaction was first described in the Vedic science texts. Our English word *creativity* also arises from this *kri*, as in "*kri*-ate-ivity."

Karma yoga: The yoga of action.

Kashatriyas: [Ka-sha-tri-yas] Literally "hurt and protect." Refers to those who serve and protect with their strength, as well as those who lead and administer society.

Kauravas: [Koo-ra-vas] The evil cousins of the Pandavas in the *Mahabharata*, led by Duryodhana. Both they and the Pandavas are descendents of a great king named Kuru after whom their entire dynasty and kingdom was named.

Kausalaya: [Cow-sa-la-ya] Ram's mother in the *Ramayana*.

Kri: [kree] Sanskrit root meaning "to do"; see *Karma*.

Krishna: [Krish-na] That Supreme Being who is so compellingly attractive that no one can resist. Otherwise called the most attractive Being.

Kuru: [Ku-ru] A great king named Kuru after whom the dynasty and kingdom of the Kauravas and Pandavas were named.

Kurukshetra: [Ku-rook-shet-ra] The famous place of battle in the *Mahabharata*.

Lakshmi: [Lak-shmi] The female counterpart of Lord Vishnu, also known as the Goddess of Fortune or Lady Luck. In Vedic thought, she is the consort, or Shakti, of Lord Vishnu and is thus the personified Source of all opulence and beauty.

Lila: [Lee-la] The spiritual activities of Divine Play that are revealed by the Avatars when they appear on Earth. These same playful activities are eternally manifest in the Transcendental realm.

Mahabharata: [Ma-ha-bha-ra-ta] One of the two epic stories of India that describes the descent of an Avatar to Earth.

Mahatma: [Ma-ha-at-ma] Great soul.

Mana: [Mah-na] Sanskrit for "mind;" applied to humans, it means possessing free will or having a mind of one's own.

Mankind: From the Sanskrit word *manusha.*

Manthara: [Man-tha-ra] The evil and hunchbacked personal handmaiden of Kaikeyi in the *Ramayana.*

Mantra: Literally a mind tool, referring to sound vibrations that are used as a pathway to direct association with Divine beings; the sound vibratory manifestation of a reality; that which delivers consciousness beyond the limitations of the material mind.

Manusha: [Ma-newsh-ya] Derived from the Sanskrit for "mind," which is *mana.* Applied to humans it means "possessing free will or having a mind of one's own" also "mankind."

Mathura: [Ma-thu-ra] The place of Krishna's birth.

Maya: [Ma-ya] Literally "not this," referring to the state of consciousness in which the atma assumes that the material reality is permanent and not causally dependent upon the Supreme Being.

Moksha: [Mok-sha] Describes the state of a soul who has become liberated from all material entanglements and is focused upon the Transcendental.

Nadis: [Na-dees] Direct current electrical healing system of meridians in the body.

Namaste: [Na-mas-te] Universal spiritual greeting that says, "I see you as a Divine Being."

Nanda: [Nan-da] Also known as Nanda-Maharaja, was Krishna's foster father in Vrindavan and the leader of the cow-herding community.

Nature: Used in three ways: material nature; Nature, as in Mother Nature; and "you are your own personal nature."

Neti neti: [Net-tee, net-tee] The process of discerning that which the soul is not, i.e., "not this, not that." Determining the soul's true identity as not being matter.

Nirvana: [Near-va-na] Literally not the possessor of anything; nirvana is *nirguna* without the reappearance of any other qualities, experiences, or characteristics. Nirvana is a kind of intermediate Moksha with no concept of self or other reality.

Niyams: [Knee-yams] The limbs of Patanjali's Ashtanga yoga that reveal the personal and internal actions and qualities that support and sustain individual practice. The conscious observances of personal action include: *shauca* (cleanliness), *shantosha* (peacefulness), *tapas* (austerity), *svadhyaya* (self-awareness), and *Ishvara-Pranidhan* (devotion to the Divine beings).

Om (Aum): [A-U-ung] This vibration of sound is said to be the original vibration that is the basis of all existence; the manifestation of eternal Brahman reality.

Pandavas: [Pan-da-vas] The five sons of Pandu. The three older Pandavas—Yudhishthira, Bhima, and Arjuna—were born to Pandu's wife Kunti by the three Devas Yamaraja, Vayu, and Indra. The other two sons, Nakula and Sahadeva, were born of Pandu's other wife, Madri, by the Ashvini-Kumaras.

Pandora's Box: In Greek mythology, Pandora's Box is the large chest opened by Pandora that unleashed many terrible afflictions upon mankind—ills, toils, and sickness—and one gift, Hope.

Prana: [Pra-na] The life force that animates all beings and is connected to the element of air; thus, the prana is sometimes called the *prana-vayu* or "life-air."

Pranayama: [Pra-na-ya-ma] Yogic breathing techniques to quiet and focus the mind, direct the life force, and prepare the yogi for the next stages of Yoga practice, culminating in Samadhi.

Pratyahara: [Prat-ya-ha-ra] The withdrawal and control of the senses. It is the stage of Yoga wherein the senses are withdrawn from their outer attachments to material objects in order for the yogi to develop greater awareness of his or her original consciousness. When this stage is reached, the seeker goes through a searching self-examination and finally confronts the source of all material desire within the heart.

Purna Avatar: [Pur-na Ah-va-tar] The full Avatar or full manifestation of Bhagavan's divinity.

Radha: [Rad-ha] The feminine counterpart of Shri Krishna. She is also sometimes called the queen of the gopis or the Transcendental Feminine Divine.

Raj: [Ra-ja] India under British rule.

Rajasic: [Ra-ja-sick] The creative guna, or state of the material energy, the symptom of which is intense desire.

Rakshasa: [Rak-sha-sa] One class of asuric beings who are sometimes cannibals and who are at the extreme of darkness and ignorance, living as they do as parasites upon the energy and life of other human beings. They are also called "the eaters."

Ramayana: [Ra-ma-ya-na] One of the two epic stories of India that describes the descent of an Avatar to Earth.

Rasa: [Ra-sa] Taste, flavor, mellows, or type of emotion that arises from a particular relationship between the liberated souls and the Supreme Person Bhagavan. Rasa is also applied to the flavors within matter that arise from different combinations of the five elements. The six flavors, or rasas, of food are sweet, sour, salty, pungent, bitter, and astringent.

Ravana: [Ra-va-na] The dark lord, or "yogi gone bad," in the *Ramayana*.

Ritam: [Re-tam] The invisible laws embedded in material nature. These rules govern all actions and reactions within matter. The Devas administer the ritam.

Ritual: To use a thing in its right way; derived from the Sanskrit *ritam*.

Romantic: Derived from the Sanskrit *Ram*. Means to rest, to sport, to be pleased, and to rejoice at.

Samadhi: [Sa-ma-di] Complete absorption in the object or subject of one's meditation, especially and finally the Transcendental reality as either Brahman, Paramatma, or Bhagavan. Through this advanced yogic state, all forms of self-realization as well as material perfections can be achieved. Becoming "the same as."

Samsara: [Some-sa-ra] Reincarnation or the repeated cycle of birth and death experienced by the eternal souls once they enter the realm of matter. Sometimes described as the wheel of birth and death or as transmigration of the soul.

Samskaras: [Sum-scar-as] Impressions and material residue accumulated over many lifetimes of action within matter. These sit on the subtle body and continue to influence behavior as habits and unconscious needs.

Sanatan Dharma: [Sa-na-tan] The true eternal nature of the atma; the soul's true nature.

Sanskrit: [San-skrit] The name of the language in which the Vedas of India are written. The word literally means "perfected," implying that Sanskrit is the most scientific and consistent language on Earth.

Sarvanamavan: [Sar-va-na-ma-van] That Great Being who is described by and who is the source and possessor of all names.

Sattvic: [Sat-vick] The harmonizing and maintaining energetic state within material nature, wherein balance is achieved for the good of all.

Science: From the Latin *scientia*, meaning "to divide"; in its broadest sense, any knowledge base or prescriptive practice that is capable of resulting in a correct prediction or reliably predictable type of outcome.

Shakti: [Shock-ti] The power of a thing that is considered female. The Shakti of Shiva is Durga; of Vishnu, Lakshmi; and of Brahma, Saraswati. The term is also generally used for the consort of Shiva, Sati or Parvati, and for the essence of any material thing.

Shudras: [Shu-draz] The working and laboring class. Those who serve and support others, as well as artisans and craftsmen.

Siddhi: [Sid-hee] "Perfection," the developed skills or talents that come in time from performing tapasya and disciplined yogic practice. There are eight principle siddhis, sometimes also known as mystic powers.

Spiritus: To breathe (ancient Greek).

Sugriva: [Su-gri-va] King of the humanlike race of apes in the *Ramayana*.

Supreme: Made up of two Sanskrit words: *su* is "a thousand times better" and *prema* is the purest, most ecstatic, most sublime, and most delicious form of love exchanged between the Divine Couple.

Sva-dharma: A person's own true original and eternal nature.

Svadhyaya: [Sva-dya-ya] The process of inquiring into one's own true nature and identity as the atma or eternal soul.

Tamasic: [Ta-ma-sick] The destructive or ignorant mode of material nature.

Tapasya: [Ta-pas-ya] From the root *tap*, to generate heat; often translated as "austerity," tapas is an action to create change in the state of one's being. Patanjali describes tapasya as one of the three activities of yogic practice, along with svadhyaya (self-knowing) and Ishvara Pranidhan (correct knowledge of the beings greater than ourselves).

Third Eye: In the middle of the forehead; opens when our ears can finally hear the eternal truth about that which is beyond our material senses and mind.

Transcendental: From the Latin *trans*, which means "to go across"; the Sanskrit *Skanda*, which means "to leap"; and *ental*, which means "to the end of all."

Unobtanium: The mineral substance the humans in the film *Avatar* were mining on Pandora.

Vaikuntha Loka: [Vy-kun-tha-lo-ka] "The planets of eternal love where no one has any anxiety or fear."

Vaishyas: [Vaish-yas] The work tendency that attracts one to business, agriculture, finance, and similar occupations. Those who have the ability to produce money, food, or goods.

Vasistha: [Va-sis-tha] King Dasaratha's spiritual advisor in the *Ramayana*.

Vasudeva: [Va-sue-day-va] Krishna's father in Mathura. He and his wife Devaki were persecuted by Kamsa for many years before Krishna delivered them by killing Kamsa. The English word *vast* is derived from the Sanskrit *vas*, so Vasudeva also means that vast and all-encompassing Supreme Being within whom all other beings are contained.

Vayu: [Va-yu] The Deva of the air element, or wind. Vayu was also Bhima's father, as well as Hanuman's.

Veda: [Vay-duh] A large collection of sacred writings originating in ancient India. They are considered to be the integral library of scriptural foundations comprising the Hindu Vedic Dharma.

Vedanta: [Ve-dan-ta] The principal branch and one of the six darshans of Vedic philosophy. The word *Vedanta* is a compound of *Veda*, or "knowledge," and *anta*, or "end and conclusion." Thus, the Vedantic darshan is concerned with the conclusion or ultimate aim of the Vedas and so deals with the precise nature of the final Transcendental goal.

Vishvamitra: [Vish-va-mi-tra] Great sage and head of all forest-dwelling sages in the *Ramayana*.

Vrata: [Vra-ta] Vow or promise. Since humans have free will, they do not act only from instinct like animals or under the ritam like Devas. Instead, they act through giving their word as a promise and thus choosing their next destination by committed action.

Vrindavan: [Vrin-da-van] Since this is the name of the place where Lord Krishna spent his childhood (age one to eleven years) it is very special to those devoted to Him as the Supreme Being. Many wonderful aspects of His Divine nature were revealed in Vrindavan. In that sacred forest, Krishna danced the famous Rasa Dance with Radha and the gopis.

Yama: [Ya-ma] The limb of Patanjali's Ashtanga yoga that teaches correct action in relation to the world. The conscious restraints of personal action are: *ahimsa* (noninjury); *asteya* (not stealing); *brahmacharaya* (sexual restraint); *aparigraha* (not grasping); and *satya* (truthful speech).

Yashoda: [Ya-sho-da] Krishna's foster mother who lived in Vrindavan in the *Mahabharata*.

Yoga: [Yo-ga] From the root *yuj* meaning "to link or connect." Our English word *yoke* is derived from *Yoga*. This idea is that through certain specific actions, one is able to reestablish one's lost link with the Supreme Beings in the Transcendental realm.

Yoga Sutras of Patanjali: A classic text on the various actions and practices of Yoga written by the sage Patanjali.

Yudhisthir: [You-dis-thir] Arjuna's older brother; head of the Pandava family in the *Mahabharata*.

BIBLIOGRApbY

Acharya, Kala, ed. *Indian Philosophical Terms: Glossary and Sources*. Mumbai: Somaiya Publications, 2004.

Agrawal, Madan Mohan, ed. *Six Systems of Indian Philosophy*. Delhi: Chaukhamba Sanskrit Pratishthan, 2001.

Arya, Ravi Prakash. *Indian Origins of Greece and Ancient World*. New York: International Vedic Vision, 2003.

Bhagavad-Gita As It Is. Translated by His Divine Grace A. C. Bhaktivedanta Swami Pradhupada. New York: Macmillan Publishing, 1972.

The Bhagavad Gita. Translated by Winthrop Sargeant. Albany: State University of New York Press, 1994.

The Bhaktirasamrtasindhu of Rupa Gosvamin. Translated by David L Haberman. New Delhi: Indira Gandhi National Centre for the Arts, 2003.

Chaitanya Charitamrita. Translated by His Divine Grace A. C. Bhaktivedanta Swami Pradhupada. Berkeley: Bhaktidevanta Book Trust, 1974.

Cremo, Michael A., and Richard L. Thompson. *Forbidden Archeology: The Hidden History of the Human Race*. Los Angeles: Bhaktivedanta Book Publishing, 1993.

Desikachar, T. K. V. *The Heart of Yoga: Developing a Personal Practice*. Rochester: Inner Traditions International, 1995.

Duneja, Prabha. *The Legacy of Yoga in Bhagwad Geeta*. Delhi: Govindram Hasanand, 1998.

Ferguson, Kitty. *The Music of Pythagoras*. New York: Walker and Company, 2008.

Frawley, David. *The Rig Veda and the History of India*. New Delhi: Aditya Prakashan, 2001.

Govindan, Marshall. *Kriya Yoga Sutras of Patanjali and the Siddhas: Translation, Commentary and Practice*. Eastman, Quebec: Kriya Yoga Publications, 2000.

Goyandaka, Jayadayal. *Srimadbhagavadgita Tattvavivecani* (English Commentary). Gorakhpur: Gita Press, 1969.

Green, Toby. *Inquisition: The Reign of Fear*. New York: Thomas Dunne Books, 2007.

Guru Pujyasri Candrasekharendra Sarasvati Svami. *Hindu Dharma: The Universal Way of Life*. Mumbai: Bharatiya Vidya Bhavan, 2008.

Harpur, Tom. *The Pagan Christ: Recovering the Lost Light*. Toronto: Thomas Allen Publishers, 2004.

Hatha Yoga Pradipika. Translation and commentary by Swami Mukti-bodhananda. Ganga Darshan: Yoga Publications Trust, 1985.

Higgins, Godfrey. *Anacalypsis: An Attempt to Draw Aside the Veil of the Saitic Isis or An Inquiry into the Origin of Lanugages, Nations and Religions*. London: Longman, Rees, Orme, Brown, Green, and Longman, 1836.

Hill, Stephen R., and Peter G. Harrison. *Dhatu-Patha: The Roots of Language: The Foundations of the Indo-European Verbal System*. London: Gerald Duckworth, 1997.

Kalyanaraman, A. *Aryatarangini: The Saga of the Indo-Aryans*. Vol. 1. Bombay: Asia Publishing House, 1969.

Klein, Naomi. *The Shock Doctrine: The Rise of Disaster Capitalism*. New York: Picador, 2007.

Kuhn, Alvin Boyd. *A Rebirth of Christianity*. Wheaton: Quest Books, 1970.

＿＿. *Shadow of the Third Century: A Revalutation of Christianity*. Whitefish: Kessinger Publishing, 2007.

Lad, Vasant. *Textbook of Ayuveda*. Vol. 1, *Fundamental Principles*. Albuquerque: Ayuvedic Press, 2002.

＿＿. *Textbook on Ayuveda*. Vol. 2, *A Complete Guide to Clinical Assessment*. Albuquerque: Ayuvedic Press, 2006.

Lockhart, Douglas. *Jesus the Heretic: Freedom and Bondage in a Religious World*. Shaftesbury, Dorset: Element Books, 2007.

Macdonell, Arthur A. *A Practical Sanskrit Dictionary, with Transliteration, Accentuation, and Etymological Analysis Throughout*. Delhi: Motilal Banarsidass Publishers, 2004.

Mahabharata. Translated by Kamala Subramaniam. Mumbai: Bharatiya Vidya Bhavan, 1965.

Mahabharata: The Greatest Spiritual Epic of All Time. Translated by Krishna Dharma. Badger: Torchlight Publishing, 1999.

The Mahabharata. Translated by Kisari Mohan Ganguli. New Delhi: Munshiram Manoharlal Publishers, 2008.

Mani, Vettam. *Puranic Encyclopedia: A Comprehensive Dictionary with Special Reference to the Epic and Puranic Literature*. Delhi: Motilal Banarsidass Publishers, 1964.

Massey, Gerald. *Ancient Egypt: The Light of the World*, Vols. 1 and 2. New York: Samuel Weiser, 1970.

Moxham, Roy. *The Great Hedge of India*. New York: Carroll & Graf Publishers, 2001.

Mudgal, S. G. *Brahmasutras: With English Translation of Madhva Bhasya*. Mumbai: Archish Publications, 2005.

Partridge, Eric. *Origins: A Short Etymological Dictionary of Modern English*. New York: Macmillan, 1958.

Pollan, Michael. *The Omnivore's Dilemma: A Natural History of Four Meals*. New York: Penguin Press, 2006.

Rajaram, Navaratna S., and David Frawley. *Vedic "Aryans" and the Origins of Civilization*. New Delhi: Voice of India, 2001.

Ramayana.Translated by Kamala Subramaniam. Mumbai: Bharatiya Vidya Bhavan, 1981.

Ramayana: India's Immortal Tale of Adventure, Love and Wisdom. Translated by Krishna Dharma. Badger: Torchlight Publishing, 2004.

Rifkin, Jeremy. *Beyond Beef: The Rise and Fall of the Cattle Culture*. New York: Penguin Group, 1992.

Schlosser, Eric. *Fast Food Nation: The Dark Side of the All-American Meal*. New York: Perennial, 2001.

Sharma, B. N. K. *History of the Dvaita School of Vedanta and Its Literature*. Delhi: Motilal Banarsidass Publishers, 1961.

Sharma, Bhu Dev, ed. *New Perspectives on Vedic and Ancient Indian Civilization*. Barre, Mass.: World Association of Vedic Studies, 2000.

Sharma, Rama Nath. *The Astadhyayi of Panini*. Vol. 1, *Introduction to the Astadhyayi as a Grammatical Device*. New Delhi: Munshiram Manoharlal Publishers, 2002.

Smith, Jeffrey M. *Seeds of Deception: Exposing Industry and Government Lies About the Safety of the Genetically-Engineered Foods You're Eating*. Fairfield, IA: Yes! Books, 2003.

Srimad Bhagavad-Gita. Translated by Srimad Krsna Dvaipayana Vedavyasa. Mathura, India: Gaudiya Vedanta Samiti, 2000.

Srimad Bhagavad-Gita: The Hidden Treasure of the Sweet Absolute. Translation and commentary by His Divine Grace Srila Bhakti Raksaka Sridhara Deva Goswami. Nabadwip, India: Sri Chaitganya Saraswatmath, 1985.

Srimad Bhagavatam. Translated by Kamala Subramaniam. Bombay: Bharatiya Vidya Bhavan Kulpati K. M. Munshi Marg, 1995.

Srimad Bhagavatam. Translated by His Divine Grace A. C. Bhaktivedanta Swami Pradhupada. Berkeley: Bhaktidevanta Book Trust, 1982.

Sri Visnu Sahasranama: Sanskrit Slokas in English. Translated by T. N. Raghavendra. Bangalore: Sree Raghavendra Guruji Centre for Divine Knowledge, 2002.

Stuart, Tristram. *The Bloodless Revolution: A Cultural History of Vegetarianism from 1600 to Modern Times*. New York: W. W. Norton, 2006.

Swami, Devamrita. *Searching for Vedic India*. Los Angeles: The Bhaktivedanta Book Trust, 2002.

Tulasidasa's Shriramacharitamanasa (The Holy Lake of the Acts of Rama). Translated by R. C. Prasad. Delhi: Motilal Banarsidass Publishers, 1988.

Varghese, Roy Abraham. *The Wonder of the World: A Journey from Modern Science to the Mind of God*. Fountain Hills, Ariz.: Tyr Publishing, 2003.

Vinayacarya, P. *Mithyatva Anumana Khandanam (A refutation of the non-reality syllogism)*. Bangalore: Sri Vedavyasa Sanskrit Research Foundation, 2006.

The Yoga Sutras of Patanjali: A Study Guide for Books 1 and 2, Samadhi Pada. Translated by Baba Hari Dass. Santa Cruz, Calif.: Shri Rama Publications, 1999.